Sunset

Sunset

A Book of Poetry and Art

Poetry by
David M. Goldberg

Paintings by
Gail Pinchot-Goldberg

RESOURCE *Publications* • Eugene, Oregon

SUNSET
A Book of Poetry and Art

Resource Publications
An Imprint of Wipf and Stock Publishers
199 W. 8th Ave., Suite 3
Eugene, OR 97401

www.wipfandstock.com

PAPERBACK ISBN: 978-1-7252-6851-7
HARDCOVER ISBN: 978-1-7252-6852-4
EBOOK ISBN: 978-1-7252-6853-1

Manufactured in the U.S.A. 06/05/20

Contents

**Painting titles are in bold*

Preface

The creation and appreciation of "Art" is a uniquely human obsession. Art exists for itself, outside of any other purpose than to arouse emotions within the individual human soul. In some sense art is a form of "Imitatio Dei". Like G-d, the artist creates ex-nihilo something of value which exists as surely as the Earth we live on. But art exists primarily in the human soul to which it is bound and from thence is transmitted to other souls who can receive it.

It is more than the specific physical manifestation—the word on the page, the note on the musical score, or the pigment on the canvas. It encompasses a total sense of some aspect of our common humanity. It is a reminder that we are human and different from the rest of nature. It is meant to transmit that which inspires from generation to generation.

We hope that you will enjoy the book.

Many of Gail's paintings can be purchased, including those shown in this book. To obtain the prices and sizes of any of the paintings please send your inquiries to **davidgoldbergconsulting@gmail.com**

When You Are Old

When you are old beyond the reach of time
And loneliness has worn away the passion of your dreams;
When age has stolen what once you were
And left you less than whole in flesh and mind;
Then remember me with but a fleeting thought,
Who knew your grace and saw you young,
Alive, amid the springtime of the world,
When all was hope and would forever be.
And know that there away in other lands,
That I belonged to you, and you were loved by me.

Beyond the Reach of Time

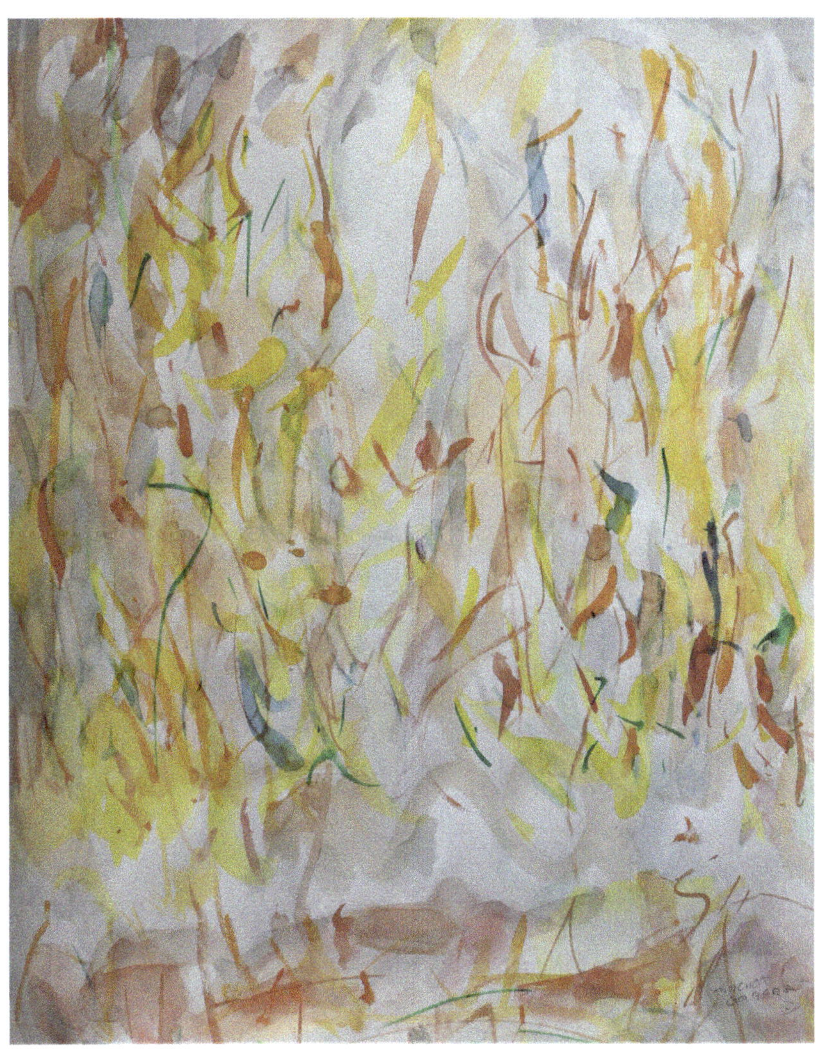

Kol Nidre 5776

To disavow a vow to G-d,
To take a sacred pledge from now
And make it so it never is
And never more could be,
Can only be a miracle,
Akin the splitting of the sea.
But only if the oath is made to G-d
Who breathing out gave birth
To time and all there ever was,
At least in Heaven and on Earth.

He made this world with great delight
But placed the snake of death inside
And gave us wills so we decide
What it is we strive to find.
Then He blessed what He had made,
But before He chose again to breathe,
He stopped to ask, perhaps in jest,
If we would make His work complete.

So we try, but cannot do;
And find we sinned along the way.
We pray for Him to stay his hand
Against sinners on Atonement Day.

"Forgive the liar and the lie,
Forgive us now at twilight time;
Purge the sinner of his curse.
To cleanse us as we were at first.
And when our lives have been renewed
Allow again this sinning Jew,
Amid tomorrow's rising sun,
To do the work that needs be done."

Menorah

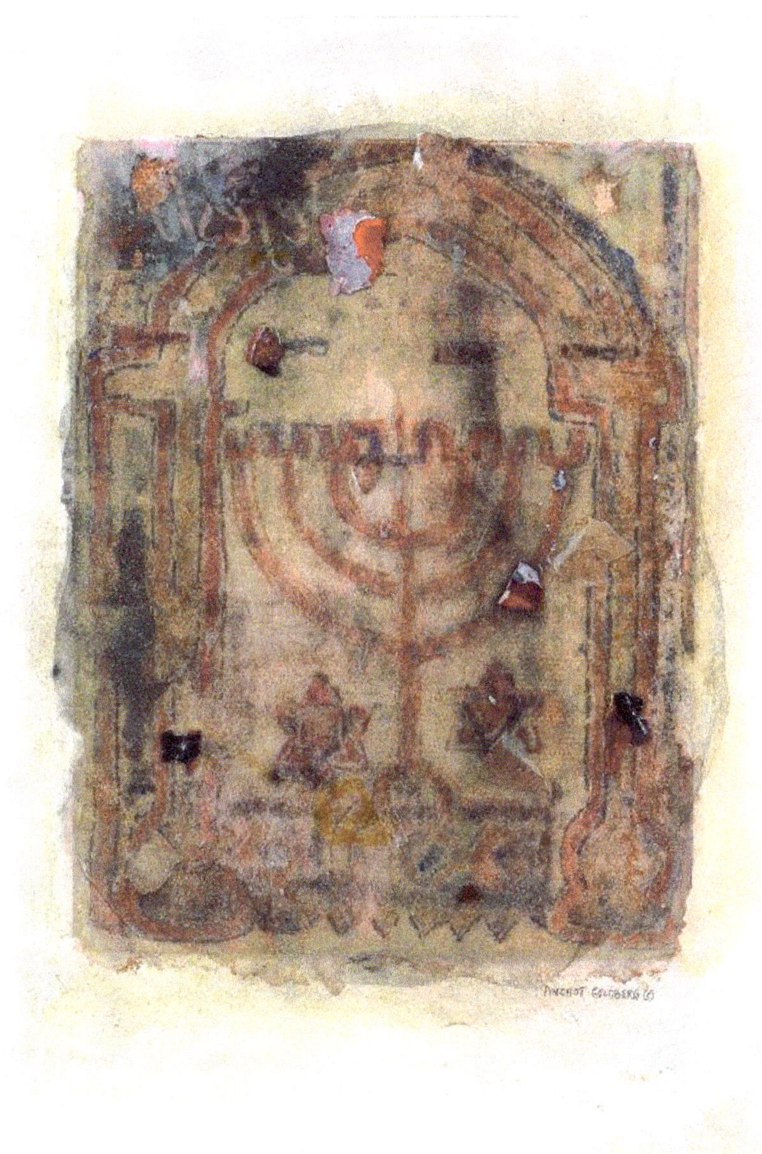

Seeking Tshuva

I lived a life which rambled on
Along some paths I did not choose,
Past some days with blinding light,
Past some chaos in the nights.

I helped some folks along the way,
Raised a family, which I love,
Had few regrets about my life,
With things I did, or could have done.

But in darker times that I had known,
Occasionally amid the din,
I found myself adrift and lost,
Committing small but venal sins.

Bubbling from forgotten pasts
These useless acts of painful hurts
Confront me as I lay awake
For those amends I did not make.

The sins were often trivial,
Mostly dull and harmless types.
Banal little stupid deeds,
Done from need or selfish spite.

A few involved some painful fights
With no one hurt beyond repair
Nonetheless they still were wrong.
They are mine; I own them fair.

A few were crimes of petty theft,
Never noticed, never seen.
Some used words like sharpened blades
To wound without necessity-
Crude attempts to force my way
Through people who resisted me.

And several times, when felt betrayed,
My anger rose 'til I was blind;
Unable to know wrong from right,
I would destroy what was not mine.

When evening comes and tides roll in,
Shadows cloud my simple dreams;
I find myself astir with guilt,
Nothing is as it would seem.

As a fly within a web
Caught in mid—trajectory;
I battle hard within myself,
But only find futility.

I cannot move against these ties;
My will is paralyzed by doubt;
My limbs are heavy, weighed with dread;
They have no strength to pull me out.

What is it that I've become?
Where is it that I must go
To clear the ledger that I have
And pay the debts that I still owe?

For reasons I can't ascertain
I feel accountings must be made,
My fate within a balance weighed
With judgment heard at end of day.

I need return what I have taken,
To make amends for what I've done,
To give to others what is needed,
To gain some peace beneath the sun.

I pray that there might be an answer.
The balance cannot stay the same.
Perhaps within the world to come
I might find another way.

Offering

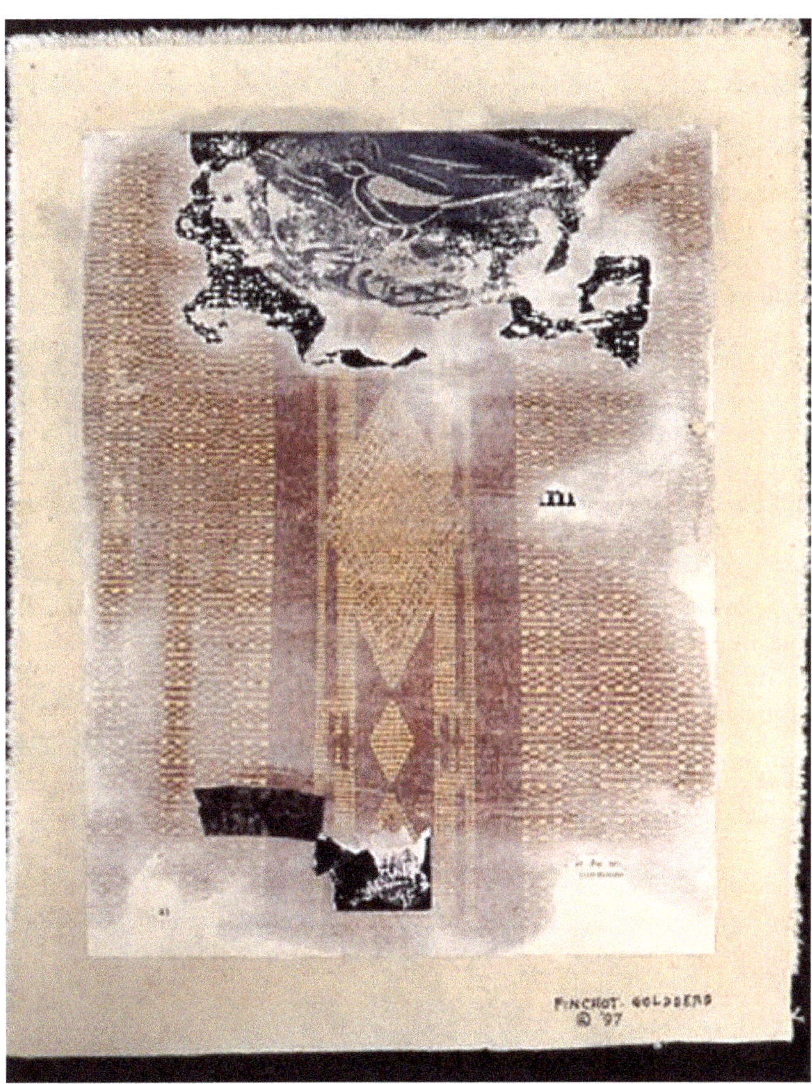

The Sapling Boy

Below the dull gray sky
The earth had died amid
The chill of winter's days.
Through a pane of frosted glass
The old man eyed the piled snows
Of yesterdays, and dreamt of times
When he was most alive
And felt the warmth of summer's light.

Recalling then a sapling boy
In spring, trying hard,
As young boys will, to fill
A void within, searching
For the man he might become.
With hope and pride in what might be,
The child dreamt of worlds unknown
That he had only just begun to try
Amid the small anxieties of life.

Girls there were, with turquoise eyes,
Whose laughter he could
Hardly understand
Who glanced at him
Amid the darkened sky
Of evening time with smiles
Meant for him and him alone.

Wanting to entice the mysteries of love
He grabbed for praise
That was not always his,
Or tried another's ways
To find if they were right for him;
But after all was said and done
He could only be the boy he was.

Because experience he lacked,
He looked to others in his pack
Of friends who seemed to know
The whys and wheres of growing up,
Like when to fight or how to ask.

Day by day the boy would learn
The paths by which the world blows
Cruel and kind upon its young.
So slowly like the sapling he had been,
He learned to bend into the wind,
Growing stronger every day,
Until the time when he could wake
And stand without another's aid
To care for those whom he would love,
And find the man whom he'd become.

Standing in the Wind

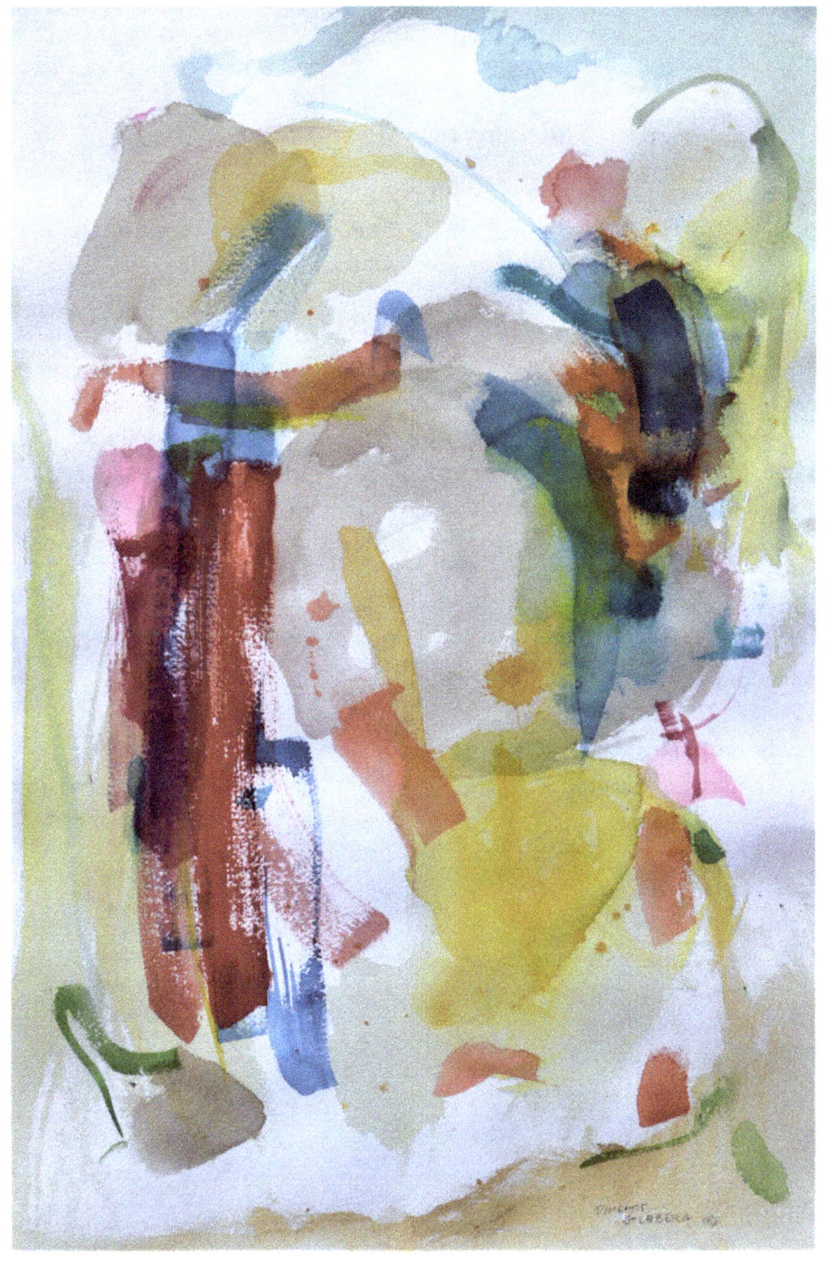

The Sparrows Made a Nest

Stick by string by straw
The sparrows came last year
In spring to build a nest
Upon a place on which
None rose the year before.

Between the downspout and the wall
The messy nest possessed
An awkward grace, formed
From bits of waste, that cradled
Three young fledglings' lives.

When the tiny birds had fled and as
The summer's days began to wane,
I used a broom as wrecking ball
To nudge the nest from off its perch;
Haunted by my guilt and shame,
I watched it flutter to the ground.

Whether perverseness of the heart
Or instinct ruled their quest,
Again, this year the sparrows
Came and claimed the spot as theirs,
Daring me to bring their home
To grief again, forcing me to weigh
The rot to house and wood
Against the joy to soul and eye.

By rules of right and might
The spot is mine. As owner
Of the house with greater size,
I know I can prevail; and for
A host of reasons justified
Will leave them homeless once again.

But why the guilt that stalks
My act? The sparrows could have
Built upon a thousand better sites
Than mine, safe beyond the threats
Of cats or hawks or brooms,
And left me free of any shame.

And yet I pray next year,
And years beyond, that they
Might still return and turn that
Empty space to awkward nest again
Until that time when I, a shadow,
Less than string or straw,
Might find myself in flight above
The sparrows'azure sky.

Lilac Lilly and Rose

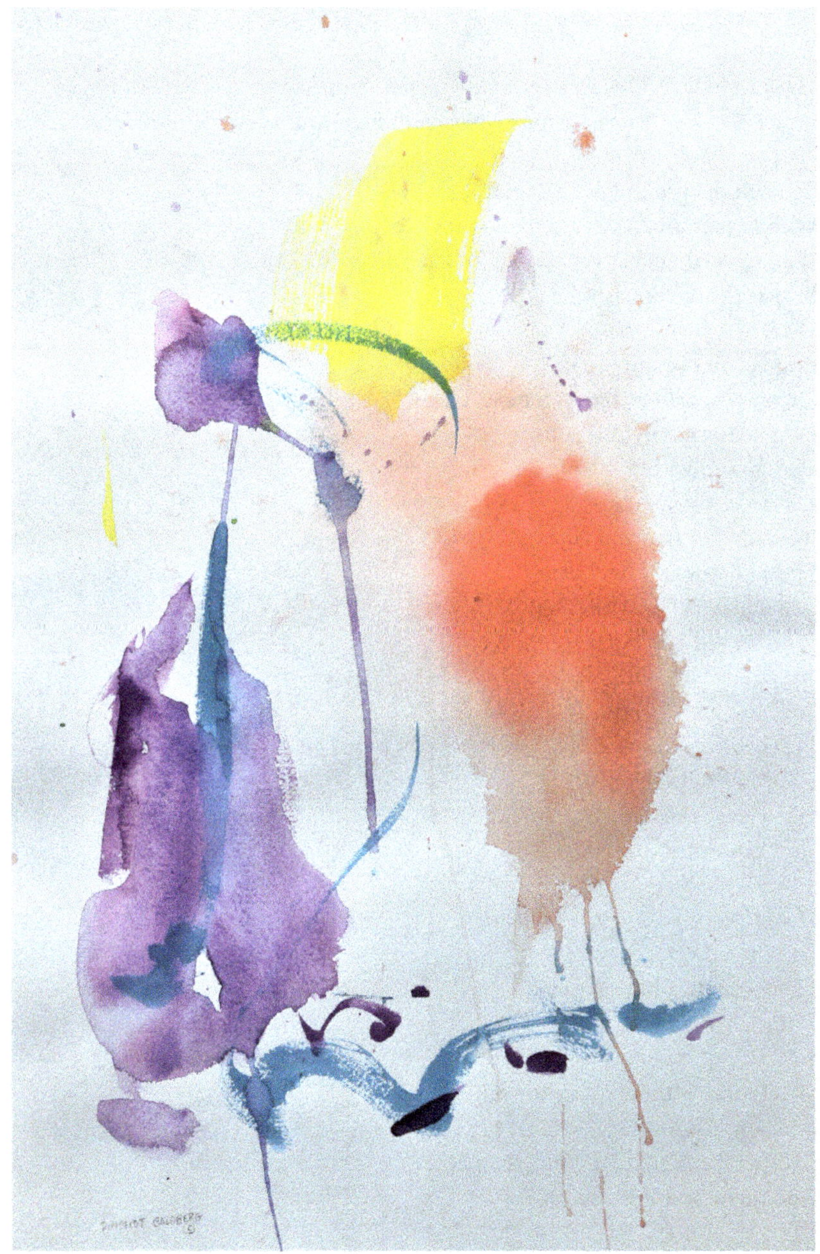

Wash 'n Toil

To a slave buried beside union soldiers in arlington cemetery in 1864
Whose tombstone reads only "wash 'n toil"

Beneath the ground of Arlington you lie
With heroes on all sides; a nameless slave
Whose weathered stone
Bespeaks our common fate.

Beside you decompose the great men
Of our land, alone, like you unsaved
Despite the strength that once
Had flowed within their veins.

It is only fair that you who had
Endured our country's evil
Should buried be with those
Who served her better soul.

For if we aren't whole
When we are grieved,
Then tide of time must
Wash away the hope that stirs,
And leave the future dust.

Heroes, cowards, slaves, we died;
It mattered not, for we will
Equal be when buried each
Within his separate plot.

What more is there to say to you
Beneath Virginia's soil,
Except "Farewell, G-d grant you peace,
And no more wash and toil."

Blues in the Night

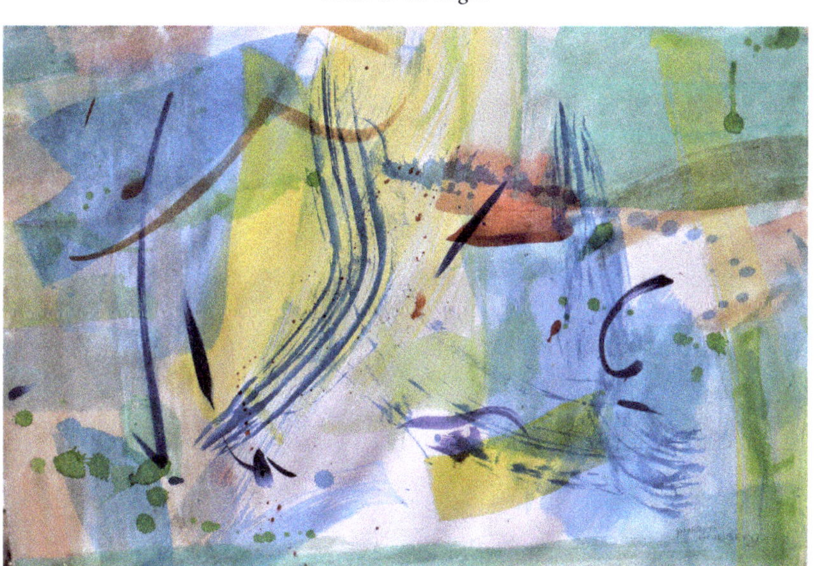

Memories in the Mist

I still see, when first we kissed,
That scene of long ago.
The rain was sweet, the world was new,
As in the mist we stood.

Let's try to love as we did then,
Without a fear of risk.
Let's seek the ways of early days
Which brought us happiness.

As time moved on, the money we earned
Allowed us to live with ease.
But as we grew old and winds blew cold,
We misplaced the love that had been.

Now I would let go of much of that time
Pursuing my dreams to be rich,
In return for that moment
In each others' arms,
Wrapped in our blanket of bliss.

At the end of our days we find we're alone.
Puzzled by where love had gone.
Did it flee with the past or dissolve in the rain
Along with the chances we lost?
Did it simply take flight leaving only regrets
In the rubble still left of our lives?
Or does it remain, that love that we made,
Waiting for us in that mist?

The Mist

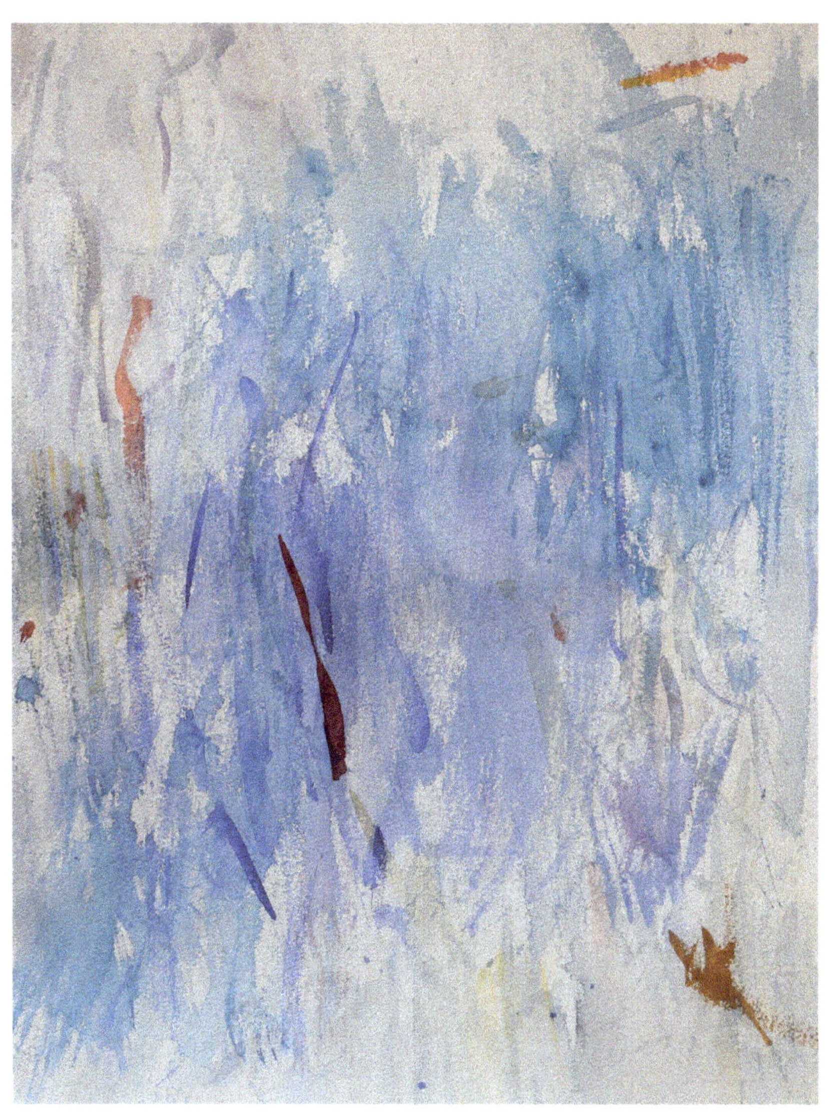

Return to Me

Do not try to touch the sun
When it's rising in the sky.
Spend the time that you are given
Finding love where e'er you are.

Too much light they say will blind you;
Shade yourself from what you see.
Take what is that you are given,
But reach for love beyond your dreams.

You my love, out there in darkness,
Find your way; return to me.
Your love waits amid the shadows;
Turn my love; return to me.

In the shadows we can find
What it is we need the most.
Searching there beyond the darkness,
Seek the love you thought you lost.

The poor man looks for greater riches;
The fool, he looks for more to know.
Spend the time that you are given;
Find a love that can be shown.

You my love, out there in darkness,
Find your way, return to me.
Your love waits amid the shadows;
Turn my love; return to me.

Sick men pray that they recover;
Sad men search for happiness.
Lonely men look for a lover,
Weary men want peaceful rest.

Find for me what I am missing;
Bring to me the hopes you have
Of days on end of sacred blessing
Of happiness that we might share.

So you my love, out there in darkness,
Find your way; return to me.
Your love waits amid the shadows;
Turn my love; return to me.

Return to Me

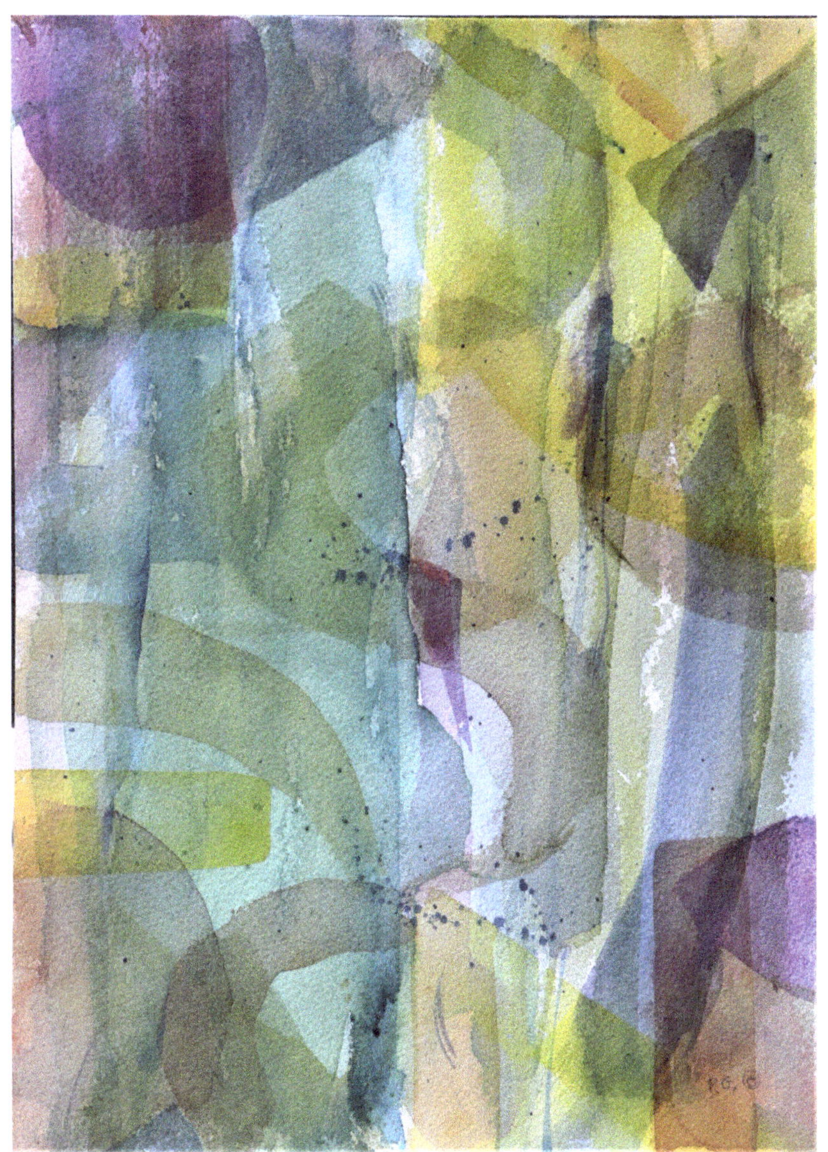

The Alchemist

In my youth I wanted more
Of all the things that money buys-
Cars and toys and fancy clothes—
Glitter that would catch my eyes.

I heard about a splendid stone,
Which would erase my poverty,
And without much effort would provide
Wealth beyond my fervid dreams.
Inspired by this tempting tale
I sailed away on violent seas.
Though looking far in search of it
The stone and wealth eluded me.

Then fame I thought, a worthy goal
A man like me might still achieve.
So I rose again to find the path
To where I thought my fame might be.
But alas the hollow cheers proved false
So I settled for the simple praise
Of a few good friends whom I had helped
And a lonely girl who could love me.

I lastly looked for happiness,
Chasing it to distant shores.
But only when I stopped my quest,
Did happiness at last find me.

In a world that's meaningless,
Add to it some friendly deeds,
Include in it some simple love
And better worlds can then take seed.

It is our choice what life might be
If we but look and understand
That we've been given all we need
To make of life what it can be.

We are more than atoms fused,
Our wishes more than vacant dreams;
Through it all we must try hard
To find those things we truly need.
Greater than mere particles
Or even endless quantum waves,
Only we create ourselves
And what it is we wish to save.

Heavenly Rain

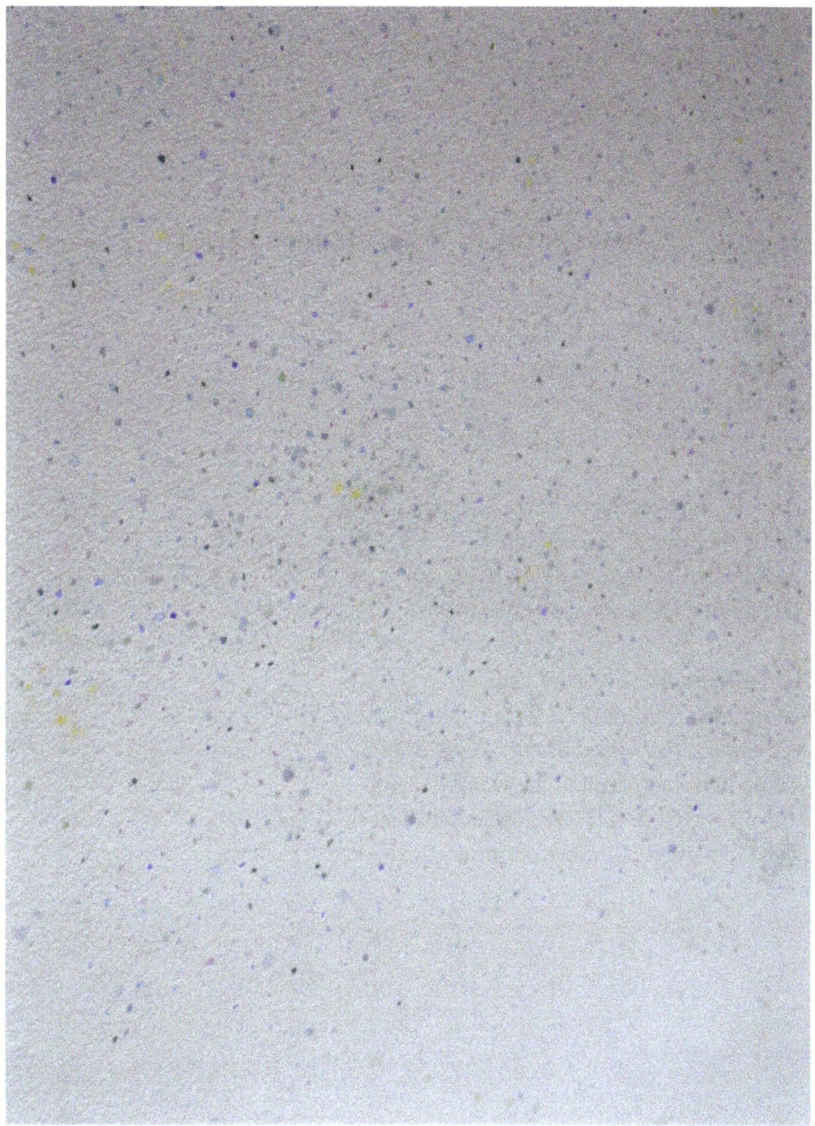

Springtime in the Ardennes Forest

The filtered light from high inside
The forest's canopy descended
In rivulets beside the aspen trees,
Dancing off the light green leaves
Until it reached the moistened ground.

There, fervid flowers, donned in royal hues,
Spread themselves throughout
The ancient battleground, like soldiers
Placed upon the earth for endless war.

Suddenly, high above the struggle,
A nightingale announced the first alarm of trouble,
As a small girl, dressed in red, the color of blood,
Waded defiantly through the wood beneath,
And snapped a flower's stem below its head,
To make a small bouquet for one she loved.

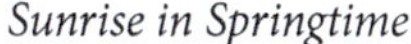

Sunrise in Springtime

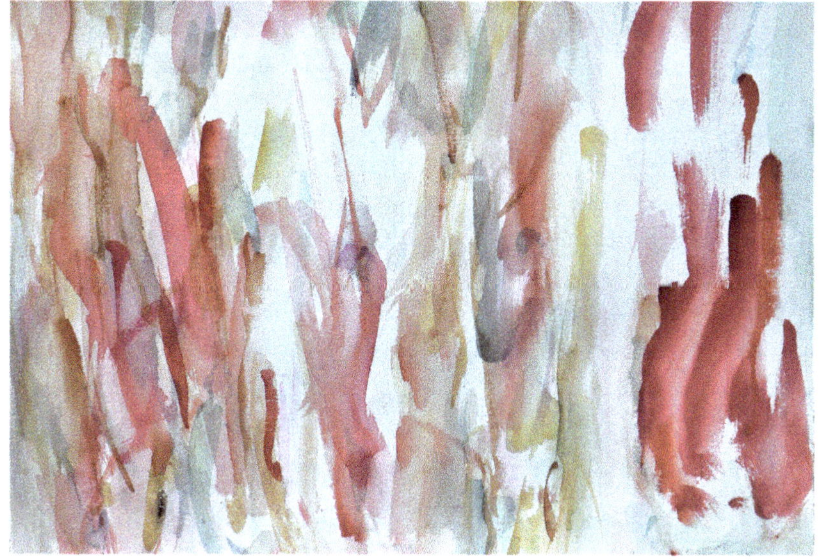

Grandchildren

Sam

The wizard waved his wand
And smoke appeared behind the curtain.
And I am left to ponder where
That smallish child disappeared
Who hid behind it
Not so long ago.
Magic it is, of this I am certain.

Else how could it be
That before me stands a man
In place of child disappeared,
So handsome, tall, and smart,
Unless through sleight of hand—
Or perhaps a miracle of G-d
Crafted with a loving heart

Alena

Alena filled with quiet grace,
Know a beauty lights your face
For which in time young men will swoon
And promise you the Earth and moon.
And even though they might be sweet
Do not give your heart too soon
Until you find that worthy boy
Who cares and loves as much as you.

You who care for many things,
Especially those with fur or wings;
Create the music and the words
Of a song that's true to you.

Let it capture all your hopes which
Reach beyond the furthest stars;
Within a life of utmost worth,
A song like that can travel far.

Love like yours creates a light
Which whirling through a distant space,
Illuminates our unsafe world
To make it one, we can embrace.
And as your light is going round
The light you make comes back to you.

So go and look within yourself
To find a space to call your own,
One to share with those you love,
A place to be forever home.

Garden in Bloom

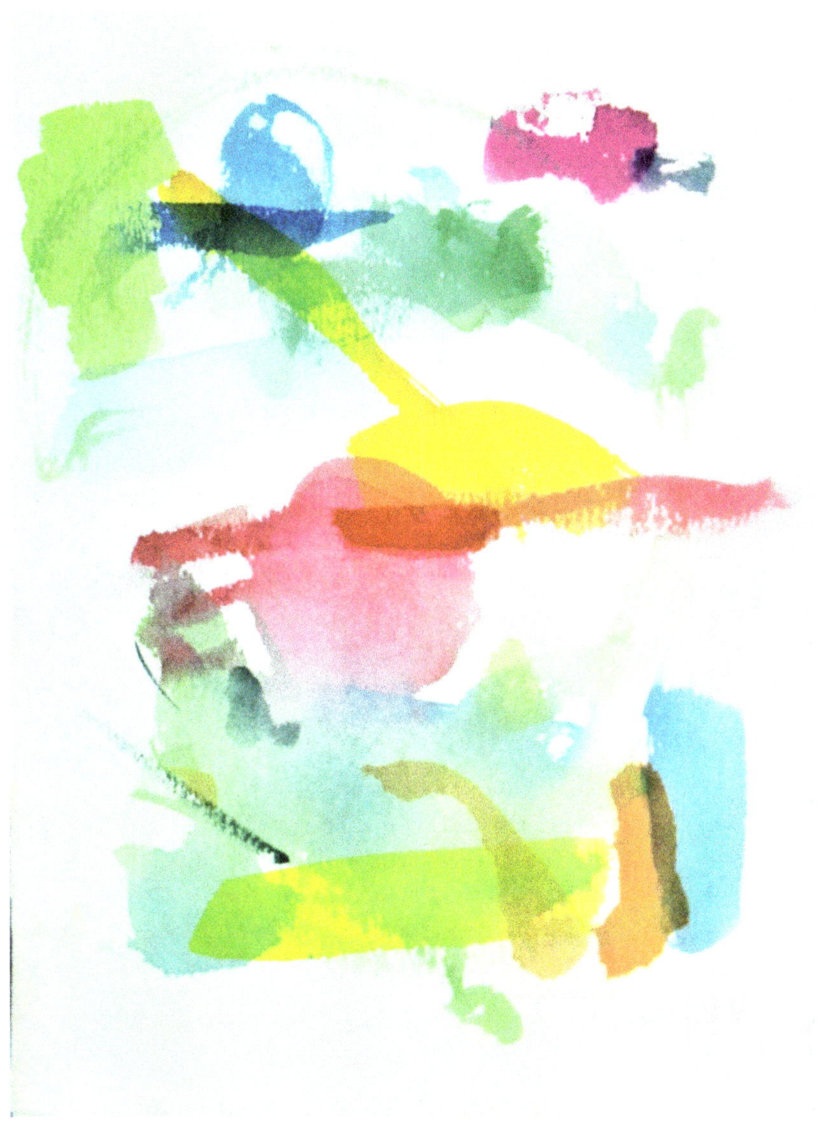

Harvest Time

Between hope and loss is harvest time,
When work to conquer weed is done.
And there before my eyes are plants
I nursed to life last spring.

With swollen fruit now dyed
In brazen hues by unknown hand,
I see tomatoes bleeding
Red through flowing vines
Astride the peppers, orange and green,
While nearby purple aubergine,
Reflecting back the waning light
Preen ripe in sweet repose;
And mocking all my early fears,
Hang tight to stem,
As if to say, "We told you so."

A just reward for time forever lost,
The fruit yields gently to my soft skinned hand
From hardened earth. And grateful
For the bounty just before the final frost,
I halt my work in moment solitaire,
As prayers of thanks rise sharply in my blood.

Garden in the Rain

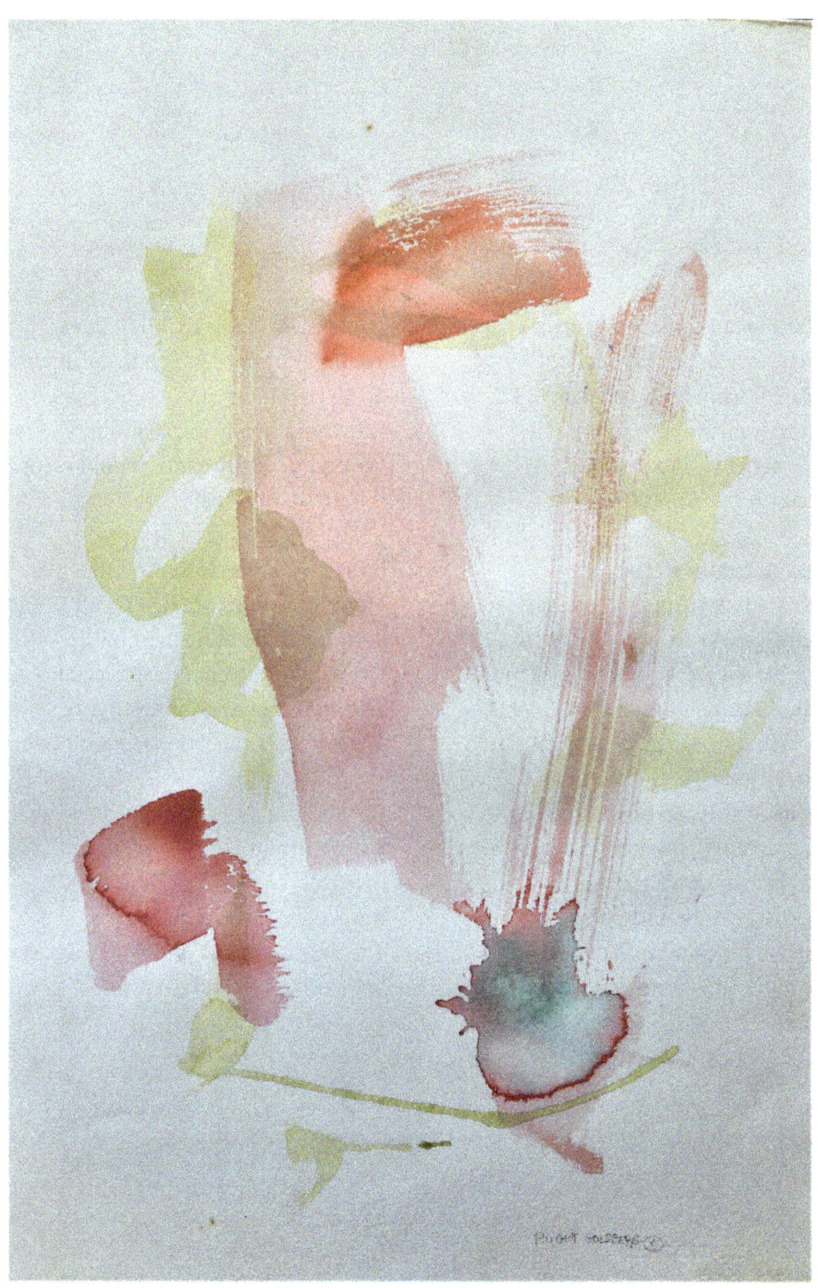

From Sun to Sun

From rising sun to setting sun
Different worlds are oft begun.
Some are born with brash displays
That find their ways to far off days;
Some emerge with quiet cries
Like baby birds about to fly.

As the sun begins to rise,
The life we have begins to change;
As it changes so do we,
From what we are to what might be;
Heroes, cowards, sometime saints
Filled with love or filled with hate.

When its zenith can be reached,
Our hopes and plans soar high and wide
For all the things we wish to do
Inside this earthbound paradise;
Some then hurt and others heal;
While most abandon what they feel.

As the sun begins to fall,
We tug the ropes which tie us down
To all the things that keep us safe.
Anchored firmly to the ground;
We dream our dreams of bold escape
Before we find that it's too late.

From rising sun to setting sun
Many worlds are oft destroyed.
Some explode in noisy shows.
Others slip through deep black holes;
The light they shed forever gone;
Their worlds' reflections found no more.

But still our sun maintains its way;
It cycles round the world we know
Bringing us both light and dark,
Innocent of what's below.
The days are short, the nights are long;
Let us go, so we might pray.

Rising to the Sun

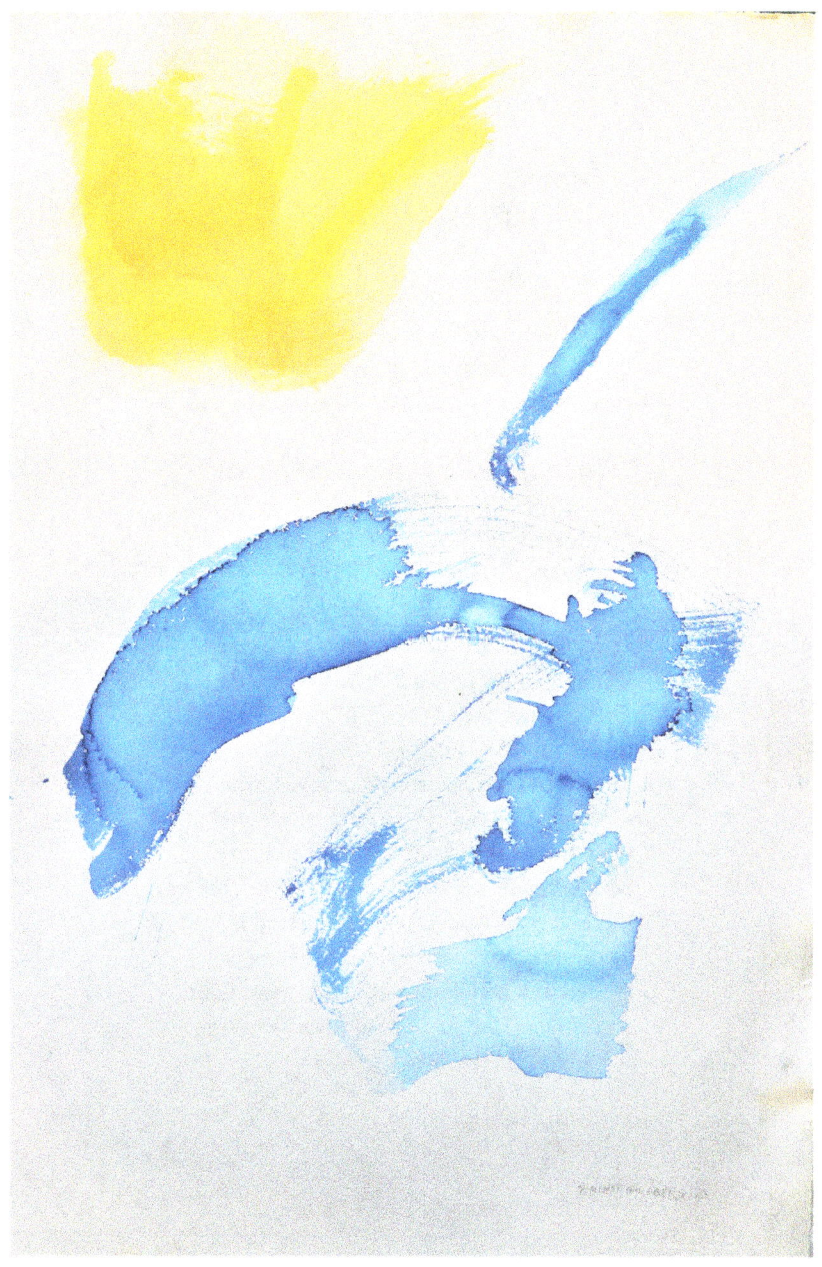

Winter Dreams

A Fugue in 2 Parts

Yesterday's men dreamt yesterday's dreams,
Winds blow cold, it's winter now.
Creating some beauty from sorrowful scenes.
The chill is in the marrow now.
Yesterday's dreams held yesterday's heat
The earth lies deep beneath the snow.
Of hate and love that will not keep.
Where is that warmth of fire now?
Yesterday's future weaved everyday's dares,
The way is covered with new formed ice.
Shaping new hopes from stale fetid air,
Our smallest steps must be taken with care.

Life keeps arriving from most everywhere.
Beyond our todays there are perils to share
Moving with caution we all need to try.
Men of tomorrow have lost their good sight.
Feeling their way through unfiltered light
Vision encrusted with both truth and lies.
Yesterday's men know why men must die.
Cleansed of the past, the Heavens will cry.

Dreams

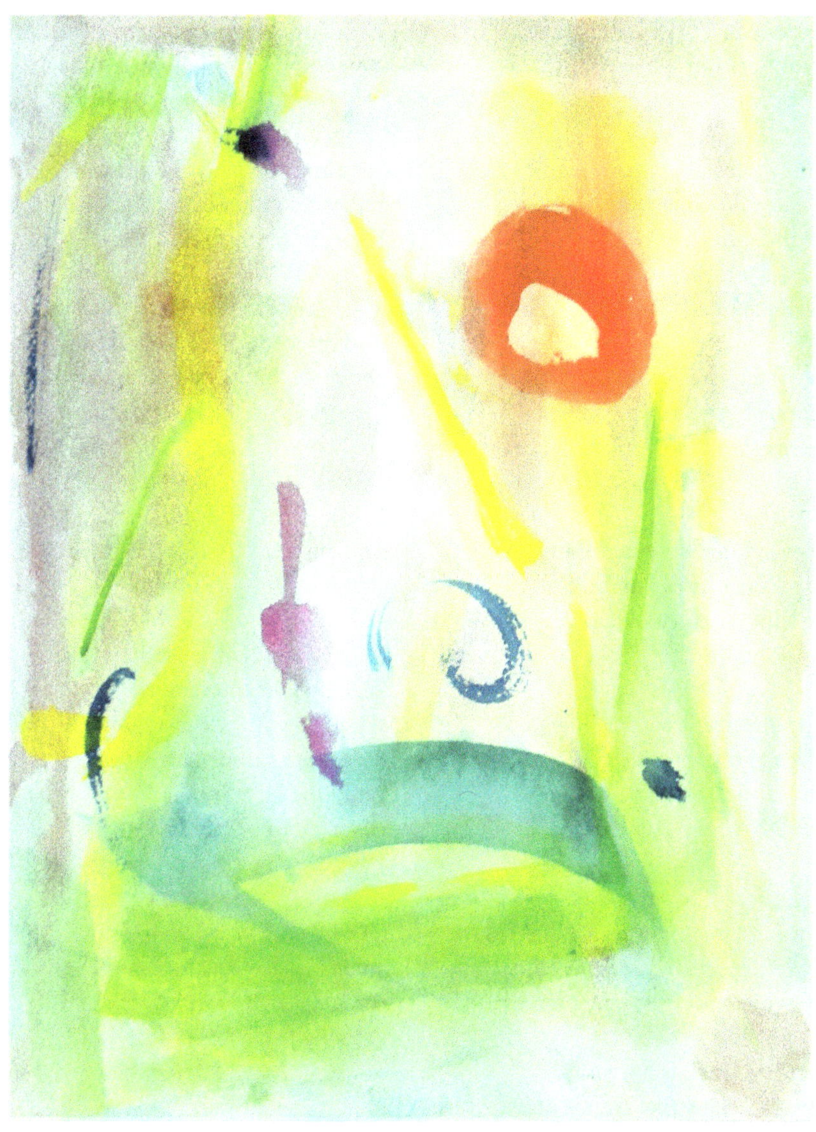

Fishing

My friends and I decide each year
To travel to some distant wood
Where we can fish in waters clear
And leave behind those petty fears
That we contend with most of time.

The sun was bright when we arrived;
We ambled down to water's edge
To see the scene and claim a boat,
Expectant with our fervent hope
Of an ample catch for next year's boasts.

The pleasant smell of summer pine
Was carried by a wafting breeze,
While rippling waves create the beat
To mark the call of forest song.

A red eyed loon went swimming by
Calling to its missing mate,
While blinding sun and dark green trees
Reflected off the placid lake.

To start one needs to tie a line
And weight it with a piece of lead
And then, in rite as old as man,
A worm to deadly point is wed.

Fishing's not quite paradise
Since things are lost as well as gained,
Disappointments mixed with bliss,
Pleasure often merged with pain.

For to catch a fish is not just joy
Though to feel it strike against one's line
Is thrilling as the primal time,
When Adam, in the Garden Grove,
Stole the fruit of sacred trees

In breathless swoon of brand new life
From under newly risen sun-
With birdsong sung and owl call heard-
Love and death all dressed as one.

When all is set for us to go
I cast my line at worlds unseen
And watch the weighted hook explode.
To panic all the fish below.

A luckless fish consumes my bait.
And discovers that his death might be
The price that he might have to pay
For stealing food away from me.

Swimming hard he tries to break
The line that holds him tight,
And attempts to shake the hidden snare
That binds his life to fate.

I slowly reel him toward my net,
Lacking pity and remorse,
When he with one last desperate try,
Breaches heaven's narrow gate
With one great leap to find
His freedom in the sky.

And there's the reason of it all
Of why each year I go to find
Some peace away from home.
For as I see his leap into the sky,
Fighting to be free of snare and lie,
Trying to transcend the chain that binds,
I know that he and I are one in G-d,
Together and untamed.

Bonaire

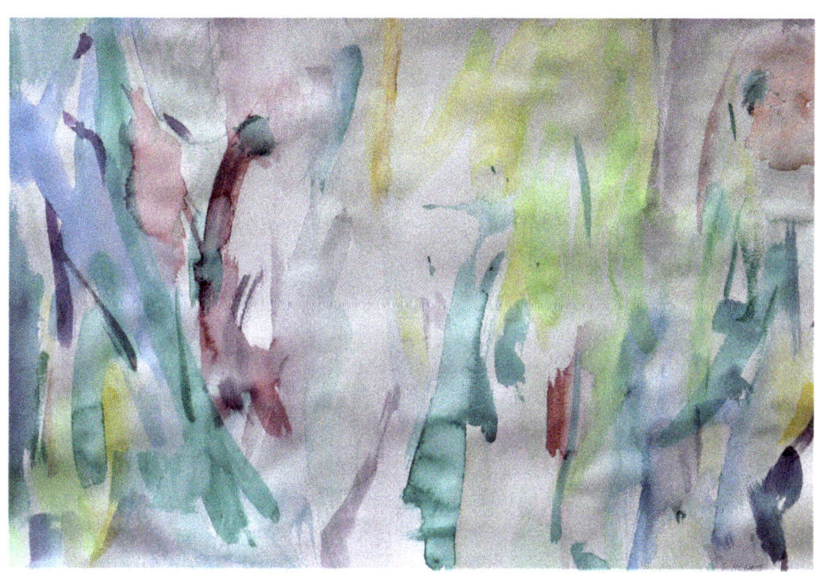

The House I Built

The house in which I built my life,
Rose brick by brick both high and wide,
Stretching out to distant lands,
Reaching out to meet the sky.

When I was young I needed space:
A spot for peace where I could dream,
A place where I might simply be
A place for songs of happiness,
A room where I might find some rest.

The rooms were built of many things,
Some of mud and some of stone;
Some were papered with my dreams;
Some were painted with my poems.

As I matured, my needs increased;
I built upon the ground I knew
A place to see my children grow,
A source from which our lives might flow,
An attic filled with memories,
A place of love which we could share,
A chapel too for whispered prayer.

In each room were souvenirs,
Mementos of the times I spent
Working hard from day to day,
Trying hard to make my way.

Through well lit corridors I strolled
Meeting all who came my way,
The rich, the poor, the kind, the cruel;
Some were wise and some were fools.

The house was built for different times
With stairs to reach those lofty heights
Where I could see, through windows huge,
The stars inside of Heaven's arc.
And each room glowed with different lights;
Some were dim and some were bright.

Old age has left me as I am;
The stairs are now too hard to climb,
The distant rooms beyond my strength;
The end I sought beyond my time.

The doors are closing one by one
Forming shadows as they swing
Across the thresholds of my life,
Quieting the songs I sing.

Is there a future for my house
Amid the world's incessant woes?
Will I learn when day is done,
If Mr. Death's a friend or foe?

Our House

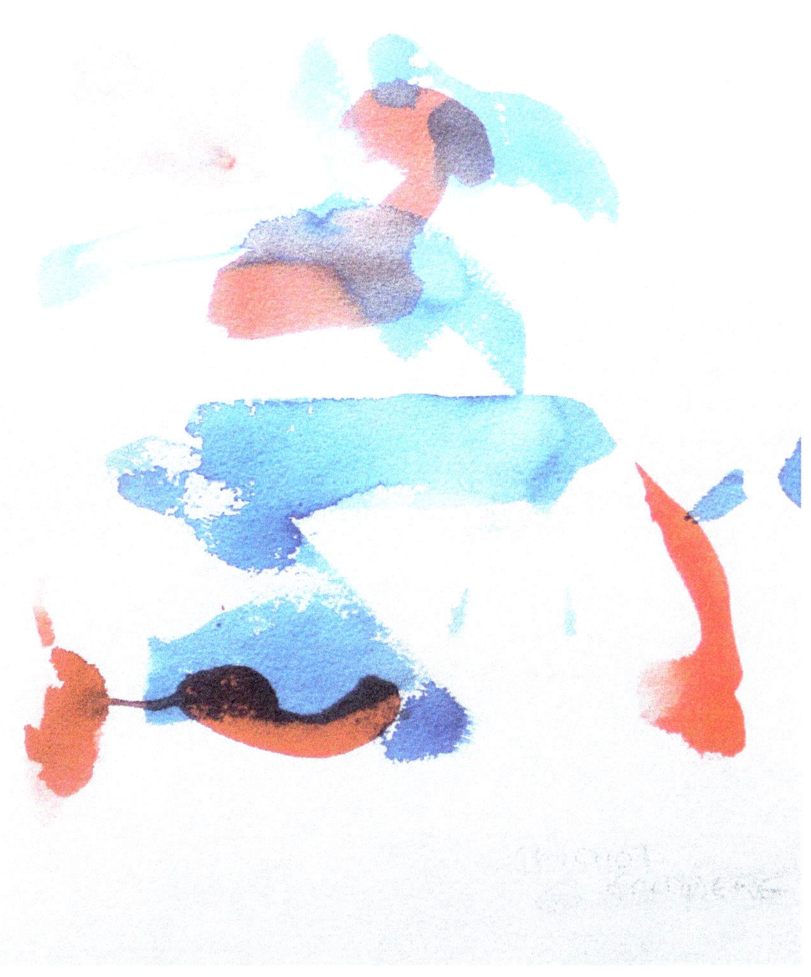

Cruising at Night

There are things that can't be seen
That blossom in the night,
Away from all cacophony,
And life that burns too bright.

Beside the rail I now perceive
That in shadow there is light,
Shimmering rays from moon and stars,
That reach the furthest heights.

The bitter pain that crippled me
To shape the sorrow that I feel,
Has briefly fled to chasms lost
Beyond the vast, vast sea.

Its absence lets me contemplate
The difference life has made
With all the hurt, with all the ache,
For family, friends, and beauty too,
And love, yes love, which I once knew.

The Captain, whom I do not know,
Has set sail to unknown shores.
Perhaps a place where we might
Thrive to continue as before;
I will not question where we'll end,
And simply trust that He
Will take us to a place of sun,
Surrounded by the bright white sand
And iridescent sea.

Across our path the winds might blow.
And storms might force us from our course
But darkness will not worry me
Because I'm now at home.

The swish of waves against the bow,
The gentle roll which cradles me,
As I stroll out among the stars
And find at last I'm free.

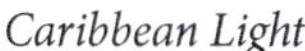

Caribbean Light

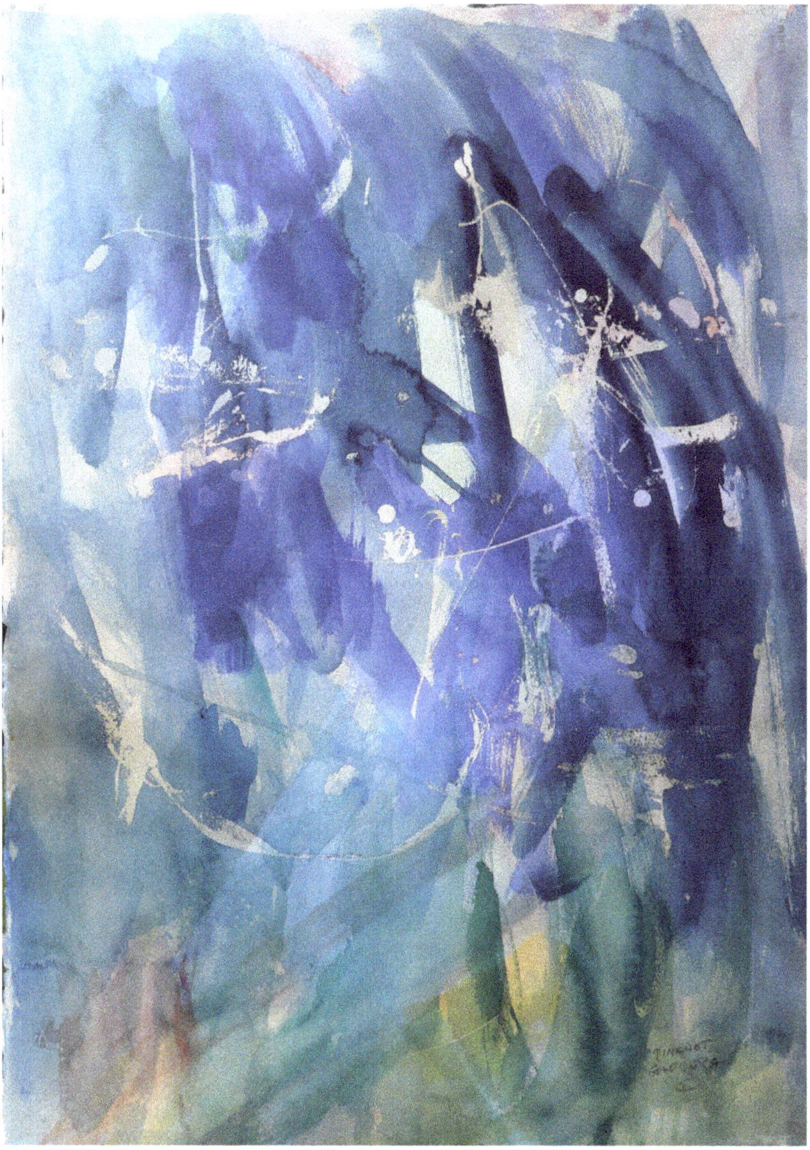

Shadow and Light

I met the dead in shadowed lanes
Who seeing me, alive and well,
Proclaimed their shock
That I was there among
The shades that lived in Hell.

I said at once," This cannot be!"
Yet, puzzled by my presence there
Where past and present overlapped
Disturbing truths confronted me.

I asked dear friends whom I saw there,
How I crossed beyond their fence
Between that world that we perceive
And the one I only sense.

They told me that the Truth
Was naught, but molded clay
Made from my thoughts;
Other truths might also be
If seen by men who were not me.

Is the cat alive or dead
Or is it simply in my head?
Can it be that all I know
Is merely that which I can show?

Below the surface there exists
Other worlds of particles
Where trees and grass
From ancient parks
Are merely different types of quarks
From which we could, if we but knew,
Build a world that's somehow new.

So what if Truth is but a lie,
With little value to it all
Except for that we keep inside.
Does that mean we shouldn't try?

Along G-d's vast continuum
Where past and future merge to one
Reality might still deceive;
But what's the choice for you and me?

Worlds whirl on in parallel
Not touching 'til their days are done.
Yet through a broad curved manifold
The dead and living meet as one.

As long as we are still alive
Seeking answers where they lie,
Probing through our universe,
We'll find a future we deserve.

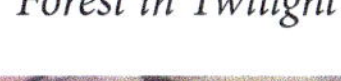

Forest in Twilight

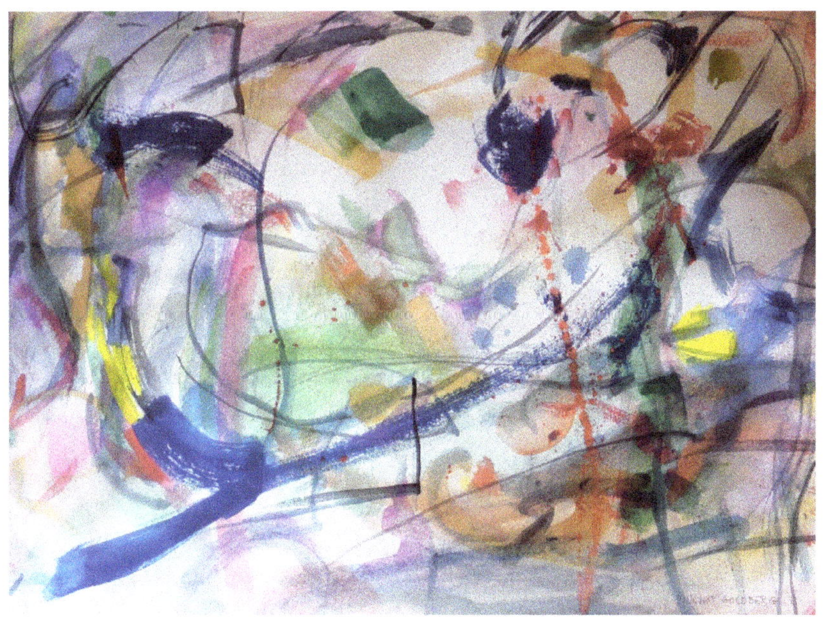

In the Park

A touch of warmth had broken through
The calloused frosts of winter's months.
From all around the children came,
To find a spot where they could play.
They scaled the heights of plywood forts,
And jumped upon the soaring swings
That rose from under winter's snows,
Like crocus in the early spring.

In the corner of the park
A carousel went round and round;
Its shadow casting dark and light
With children jumping off and on.

The watchful eyes of wary moms
Ensured their children met no harm,
While other elders stood around,
Bundled up in knitted scarves,
Speaking to their passing friends,
Discussing all the latest trends.

I came upon this pleasant scene
Remembering a prior day
When I would bring my children there,
To let them run and watch them play.
We were young and did not know
That life would race as we grew old.
The future stretched out endlessly;
Our dreams encompassed everything.
All was promise, all was hope.
We reigned as if immortal kings.

From the corner of my eye
I spied two lovers walking by,
Holding hands as lovers will,
Unfazed by all the children's cries.
Once again my mind flashed back
To former times when love was free
Without a price that need be paid,
Or so it seemed that way to me.

The shining sun began to fall;
The carousel kept round and round,
With children, flying off and on,
Their crumpled coats upon the ground.
On a bench not far away
I sat there leaning on my cane,
Surprised at how the world could change,
And manage yet to stay the same.

As daylight rays began to fade,
In the air a chilling breeze
Pushed away my reveries
And told me it was time to leave.

But I can hear within my head
The carousel still going round,
The steady beat of children's feet
Slipping off and leaping on;
And I have come to understand—
What had been lost might still be found.

Whisper softly memory
The hopes and lies of yesteryear;
Whisper in my failing ears,
Whisper whom I still might be.

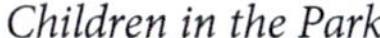

Children in the Park

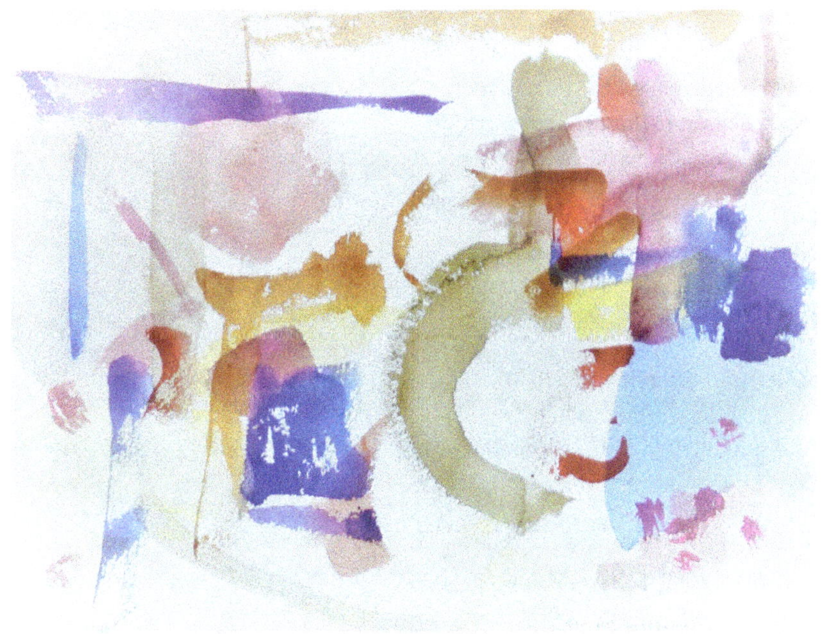

String Theory

The entire world is made of strings
That vibrate as the violin sings,
Creating stars and lovers' sighs,
Infusing beauty in our lives.

The waves respond to throbbing winds;
And souls no doubt will also sing
In resonance to what they find—
Be it light or eagles' wings.

The beauty which we hear and see,
That reverberates with you and me,
Is nothing more than all those strings,
Creating wondrous harmonies.

But within the music that we make
Notes can sound with dissonance,
Since all the conflicts we have made,
Can leave our lives a bit unstrung.

Strings can sometimes be too taut
Creating noise a bit too high
And tunes will sometime lose their way
Because of notes that went astray.

But wayward strings and melodies
Can be retuned to sweeter paths,
If we but seek their harmony
And leave the clatter in the past.

So listen close to all around
And find a way to resonate
With all the beauty that you feel
And all the beauty we create.

Through our lives the Fiddler bows,
So we can find a song to love
Which once it's merged in symphony
Completes the music He'd begun.

Serenity

Alan Turing

Alan Turing wished to know
What it was that made us so
Much smarter than those things,
Like bees and birds that fly and sing,
Or even tools which buzz and whirr
With motors, tubes, and wiring.

With nothing more than rules and codes
He conjured up a thought machine
To answer doubts from queries posed
About the **what** of everything.

Important answers did he find
To questions that he had in mind—
Like how to make an airplane fly,
And what might be the root of pi,
Of when to hold and when to share,
Or which to eat—the plum or pear?

He saw his gadget on the brink
Of something quite incredible.
And with a faith, a perfect faith,
He began to say that it could think.
He thought the Truth of everything
Was now within his fingers' grasp,
And replicating Adam's sin
He sowed a small and whirling wind.

Gödel knew and even proved
That there are truths unprovable;
But Alan would not stoop to seek
A truth that only hearts might see.
But with his heartfelt certainty
He discovered that the world could be
A great deal crueler than need be.
And dismayed by input of this sort
He looked at life with great unease.

So he queried his smart machine
Of **WHY** it is that we should be.
But despite the logic and the rules
His machine could only whirr and purr
And could not find the answers which
would soothe his vast anxieties.

Without the answer as to "**WHY?**"
With little love, with nothing right,
With only pain awaiting him,
His rules of logic said "to die."

So, trapped by what the logic said,
A poisoned apple by his side
Turing tasted of that fruit
Which he had nurtured until ripe
And closed his eyes and swallowed hard
And lost his chance at love and life.

How It Was Learned

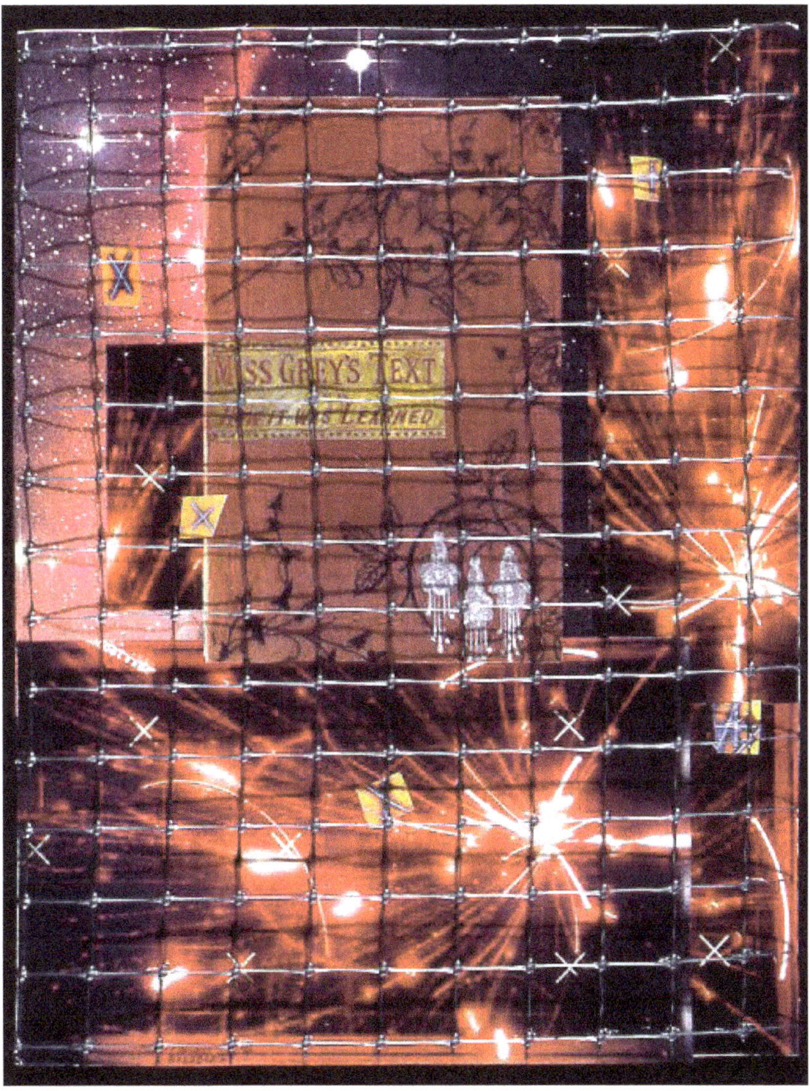

Backyard Beauty

The sight of nature close at hand
Gives to me a sense of peace-
Giving me a chance to breathe.
Filling a small primal need.

But age has sapped the strength I had;
I tire much too easily;
Throughout the day, I struggle hard
To keep exhaustion far from me.

No more for me heroic hikes
Through river valleys lush and green
Or safaris made to Africa
To explore a world that's still pristine.

But every loss creates a gain;
And growth is found where change is
  made.
Despite my more restricted ways
I've found a scene I would not trade.

I came across a Walden Pond
Just outside my kitchen door,
As perched upon my backyard porch
I gazed upon the sight below.

Bird and beast from many points
With hopes and hunger came to feed
Upon the ground my wife has sown
With corn and fruit and sorghum seed.

The squirrels and chipmunks, cunning
  thieves,
Cautiously approached the spot,
Pushing past the smaller birds
To eat whatever food they want.

The doves dressed in their finery,
Cooing to their nearby mates,
Strut around my little plot
Looking like they own the place.

A host of sparrows flutter in,
But startled by a noisy breeze
Rise as one upon their wings
To hide and cry in distant trees.

The robins scorn our humble fare,
But find the bath we left for them;
Splashing to their heart's content,
Spewing water everywhere
Making fountains in the air.

A bright red cardinal starts to sing;
He whistles with staccato fades.
Rabbits simply wander through
To nibble grass that's in the shade.

A parade of others come our way-
A butterfly rests on our fence.
A redwing blackbird passes through.
A possum lopes to who knows where.

And once we had a hawk come by
Who cast a shadow six feet wide;
And all the other creatures there,
On sensing it, were terrified.

There's magic in these simple scenes
That imposing mountains cannot teach—
A single flower on a fence,
A bird that sings in early spring,
A butterfly upon the wing,
The scent of rain upon the wind.
The smile of a loving friend,
Day's promise of a peaceful end.

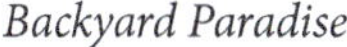

Backyard Paradise

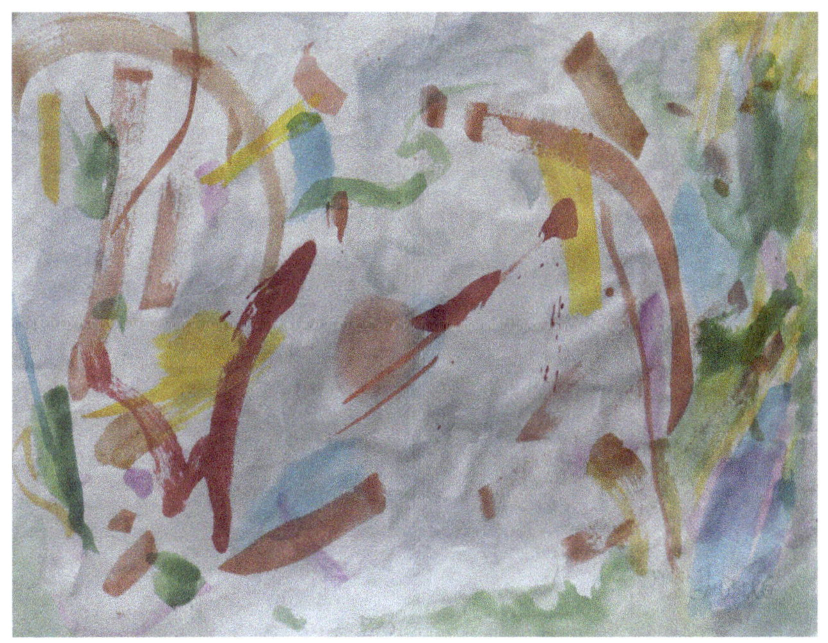

A Friend's Reprieve

The maple tree within our yard,
Which stands as sentry to our home,
For forty years protected us
From wind and sun and thunderstorm.

He towers high above the ground,
Seventy feet at my best guess;
Though rarely making any sounds
His specter is our constant guest.

Between his height and girth around
I estimate that he might be
Perhaps, as old as eighty years,
A venerable age for maple trees.

The tree was there before the house,
Sprouting first on marshy fen.
He somehow dodged the builders' saws,
As workers cut down nearby friends.

Storms have taken major tolls,
Like lightning strikes ten years ago,
Which sheared away a major limb
That left him standing gracelessly
Bereft of nature's symmetry.

The wound exposed his inner wood,
A place where bugs which bring disease
Can burrow underneath his bark,
To dine with a voracious greed.

But despite this loss of loveliness
Birds and squirrels and other things
Ignore the damage happily
To play within his canopy.

My landscape gardener said to me,
Those trees like him should be cut down,
Making room for younger growth;
Without much thought I turned him
down.

For I have reached those promised years
Which G-d allots to average men;
And I have felt cruel nature's sting
That left me hurt on broken wing.

Everything deserves a chance
To seek a life that it finds best,
To venture up toward greater heights
Despite a past which scars its flesh.

Survivors from a different time,
Bending when we have a need,
Standing firm against the winds,
We're still here—my friend and me.

Confetti

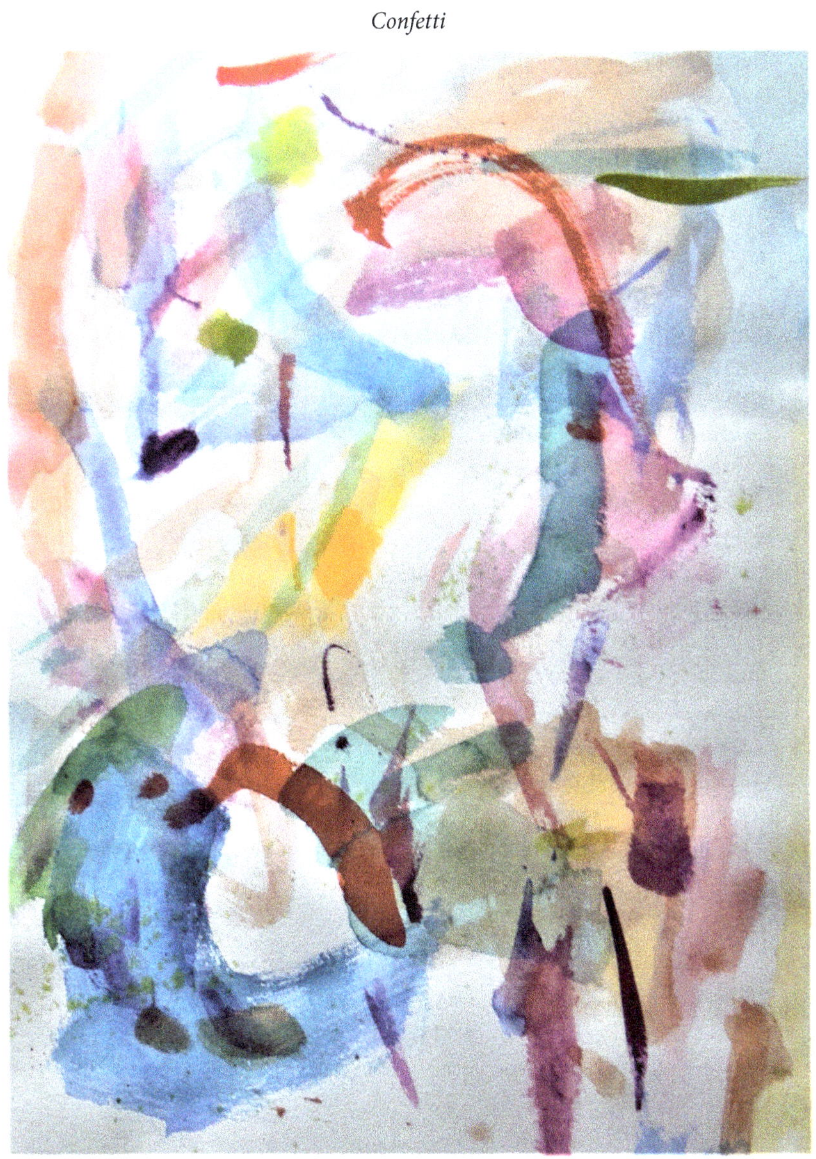

Sonnet for the End of Time

Between the facts and lies which haunt our lives
Are little cracks which open up to skies
Beyond the stars, where all is clear.

There beyond our noisy sphere,
Where truth cannot be seen or heard,
A stillness reigns where only G-d
In mystery remains. And we are
Nothing but a part of He who does
Encompass all there is and evermore will be.

Illumined by that Light that blinds us to ourselves,
We lose our sense of what we've ever known or been
And then, and only then, we truly know, the meaning to be free.

Between the Stars

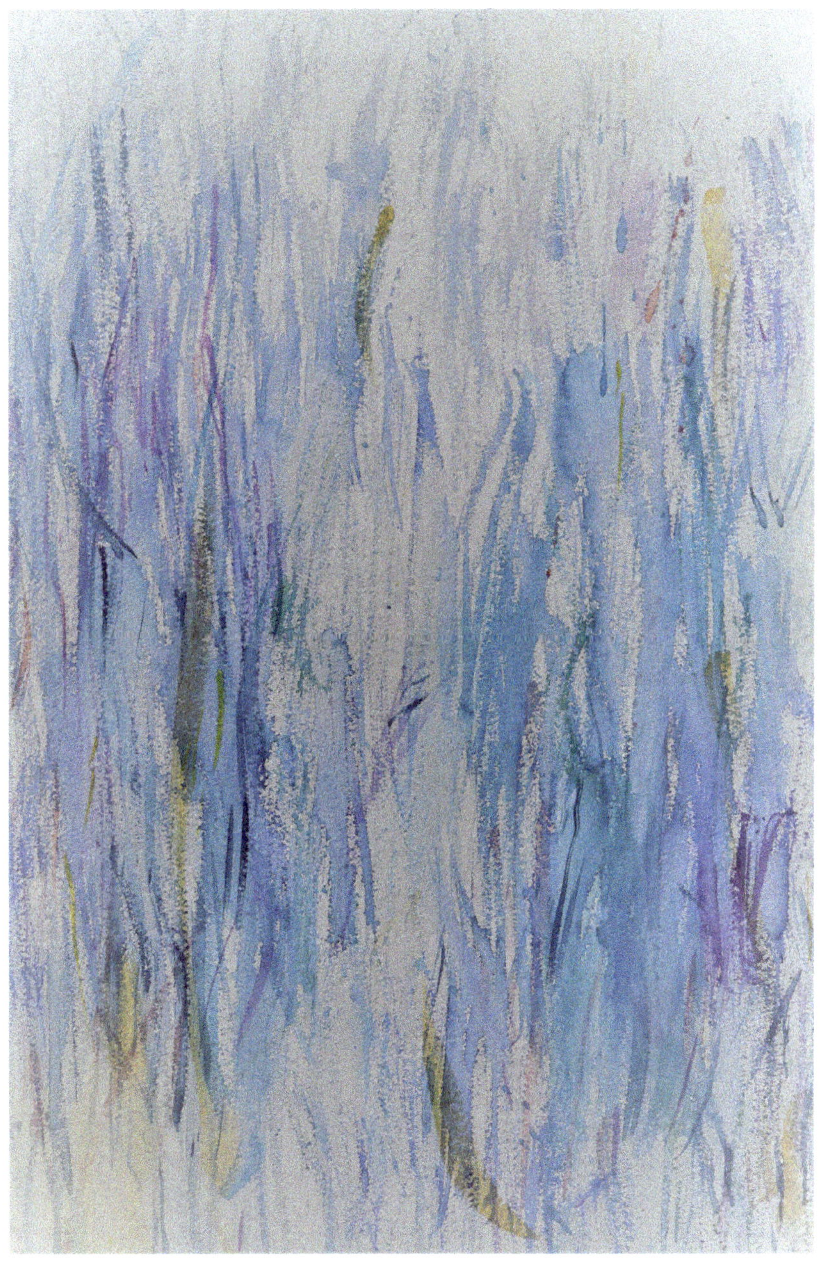

The Grass

(For my friends Matt and Nancy Diggs)

When light first breached the darkened sky,
A hot relentless sun began to rise
And parch the land until
It cracked the shallow crust
That opened slightly for the seed
To find its way, allowing rain
To flow in crevices unseen,
And with the moistened dirt,
Cajole the seed to life.

The grass grew tall, unturned by plow or spade;
And in the summer wind it waved,
Green with hope and promise barely made,
Redolent with all those scents that life creates.

But that was many years ago. The grass is gone.
In winter's time it died, drowned beneath
A snow that covers all. And in its place is memory
-A trade perhaps unfair-but still a trade that leaves
Us richer than before the grass had grown,
With dreams of years we never owned.

There are no answers to the riddle posed
Except what G-d has granted us to know-
That life and love will still survive,
Because the spring will once again arrive
As we await the melting of the snow.

Dreams in Winter

Moses on Nebo

Alone on Nebo the old man climbed
A stony path toward journey's end.
With anxious mind he hoped to find
A way his troubled heart might mend.

Freed at last from duty's weight
But burdened by his memories,
He found himself condemned by G-d,
For reasons of necessity.

Born a slave, adrift at birth,
No place was home; no home was his.
And now at last when home was nigh,
The home he sought had been denied.

Unsure of what it all had meant,
Those years of work with sacrifice,
Too little wage had he been paid
To make up for his banishment.

The blood red sun began to set
Diffusing light across the sky.
The old man sensed the aching dread
Of dying men bereft of time.

Glory was not what he sought.
What he wanted, nothing more,
Was just to know that those he'd led
Had found themselves secure and fed,
Settled in that goodly land
With a simple peace that he might share.

On top of Nebo the old man saw,
Despite the dimming of the light,
The mottled shadows on that plain
For forty years he'd sought in vain.

Denied the entry earned by right,
Despite good faith upon his end,
This punishment, devoid of crime,
He struggled hard to comprehend.

Because he had controlled their fate
Respect and fear had been his due,
But now that he was at the end
He needed more from those he knew.

Perhaps he'd steal some extra days
With all those children whom he reared
So in the future he might hear,
They loved the man who brought them there.

But love is not conjured from air,
Nor formed in light by stark decree,
Because true love is never gained
Except through reciprocity.

Alone on Nebo the old man heard
An echo from a distant place,
The rustle of a gentle wind,
Where G-d found him, and he found grace.

He sensed a breeze upon his back;
No longer standing there alone,
He looked around a final time
And knew that it was time to go.

In the end he understood
And prayed to G-d a final wish,
Released his soul for Heaven's sake
Then rose to Heaven on His kiss.

Red Sun

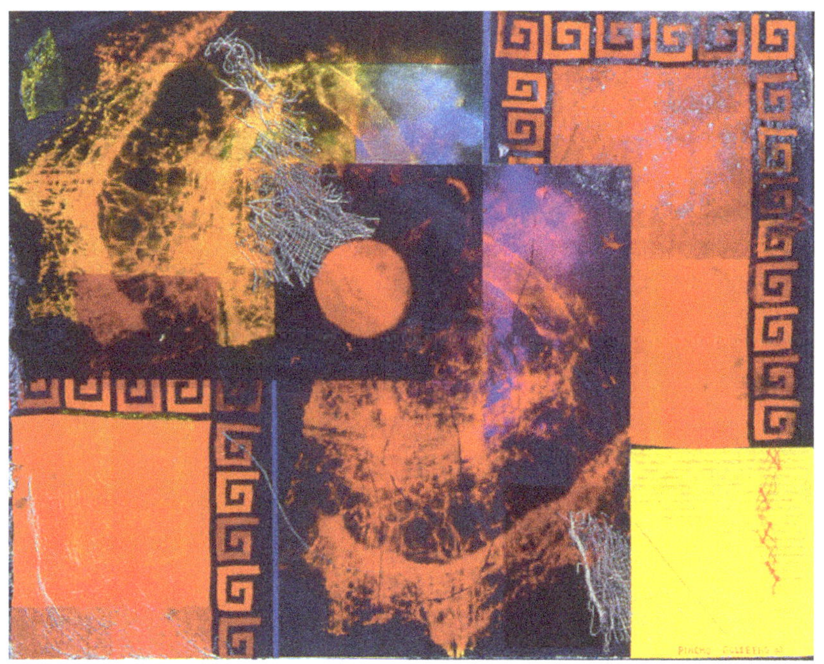

Kensington Gardens

In Kensington Gardens the sun would shine,
Reflecting off the babies' prams
That nannies pushed in 4/4 time
While all around them children ran.

In Kensington Gardens the flowers showed
The muted colors of autumn air,
As young men pranced between the rows
Of long limbed girls with silky hair.

In Kensington Gardens the grown men sailed
Their little boats across Round Pond,
While racing boys would launch their kites
Aloft to winds that drove them high
Above the green receding ground
With tails a' dancing in the sky.

And In Kensington Gardens the old men sat
On wooden benches where they could see
The shadows of their distant pasts
Where they could run and prance and dream.

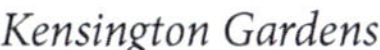

Kensington Gardens

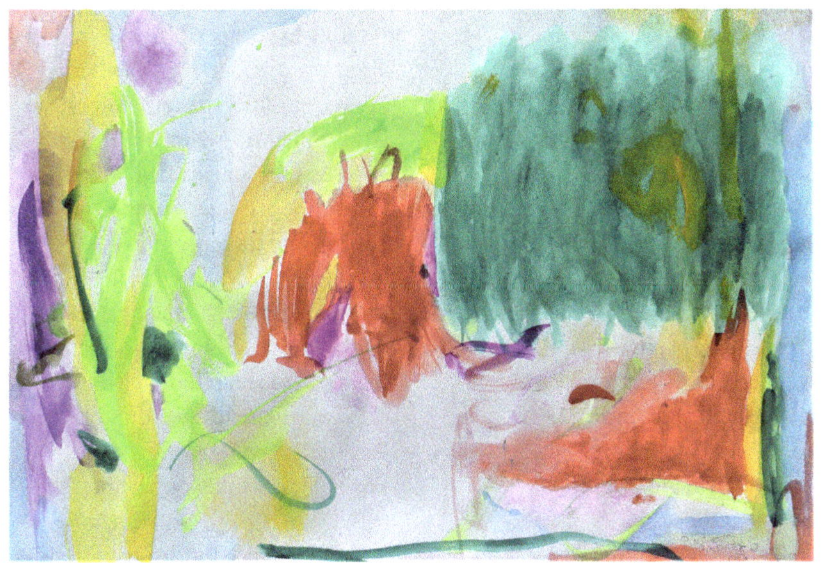

Upon the Serengeti

First light dawned upon the Serengeti
And Eden broke anew with life reborn.
The sun, more sensed than seen,
Spun out its luminosity in streaks
Of red and orange across the sky,
Revealing far and wide the weightless
plain,
While life began to quicken once again,
Beneath its seeing eye,
As grasses waved in time
To rhythms of the morning breeze.

A lone acacia tree in which
A leopard spent the night,
Rustled gently as its guest
Began to rise; the lissome cat
Arched its back and falling
Fluid as a waterfall to ground,
Began to scan the tall
Savannah grass with hungry eyes.
Moved by instinct and by need,
Devoid of pity for its prey,
It searched for life on which to feed,
Upon the Serengeti.

A hundred yards away, created
From the flames of ancient times,
A kopje stood—A sentinel
To birth and death through ages past.
Near its base, a small gazelle had come
To graze, as graceful as a ballerina
High en pointe, she raised her head
And sniffed the wind. but smelling
Terror in the air, she fled
In fear toward safer ground
And swiftly disappeared.

The leopard watched her get away
And shook its head, as if it did not care.
It turned in studied nonchalance
To wander carelessly around the tree
And settled in its shade to wait
For other prey this perfect day.

Another chance for death and life
Would surely be, as the sun rose
Higher in the sky, upon the Serengeti.

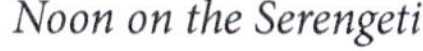

Noon on the Serengeti

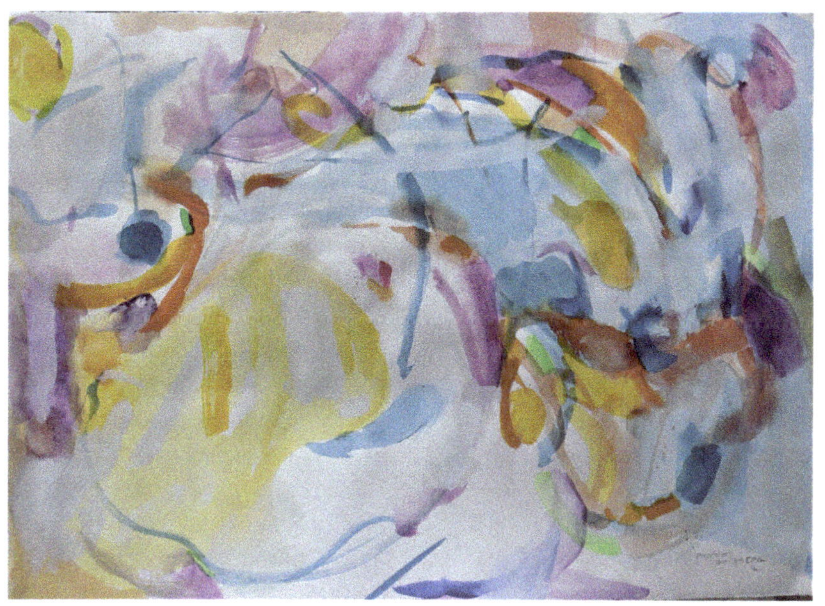

Seder

Our fathers swore a sacred oath
That if our G-d would make us free,
We would pledge Him fealty
With gratitude and piety.

Freedom came uneasily.
Midst wars and plagues on desert sand,
They stumbled toward a distant place,
Protected by His unseen hand.

Many died along the way;
Others loved and life renewed.
Time flowed out from hidden streams;
In the end, His word proved true.

Past forty years of wandering
They sat along the Jordan's edge
Remembering the times behind,
Staring at the years ahead.

From all descendents who survive
Without the stain of slavery,
To He who gave us saving faith,
These oaths and debts must be repaid,

But how to swear if we weren't there
Or comprehend what they were shown?
We need to conjure up the past
To understand what they had known.

We'll hear the tale of Hebrew pain
And break the bread of poverty,
We'll eat the bitter herb again,
Creating tears of slavery.

Our children too must do their part
With riddles asked in simple tunes,
So they can sense what went before-
To learn the reason they are Jews.

Recall the voice of Joshua
Who told us that we have to choose
Who it is we wish to be,
What to gain and what to lose.

Though foes and friends
Will sometimes change,
While joy and sadness alternate,
Every year we come anew,
This covenant to celebrate.

Amidst the burdens of or lives,
Every year we must affirm
That He is ours and we are His—
A simple act of love returned.

As past and present merge to one,
The future's shadows can be seen.
What was destroyed will be rebuilt
By bricks and straw on ancient dreams.

To Tell the Tale

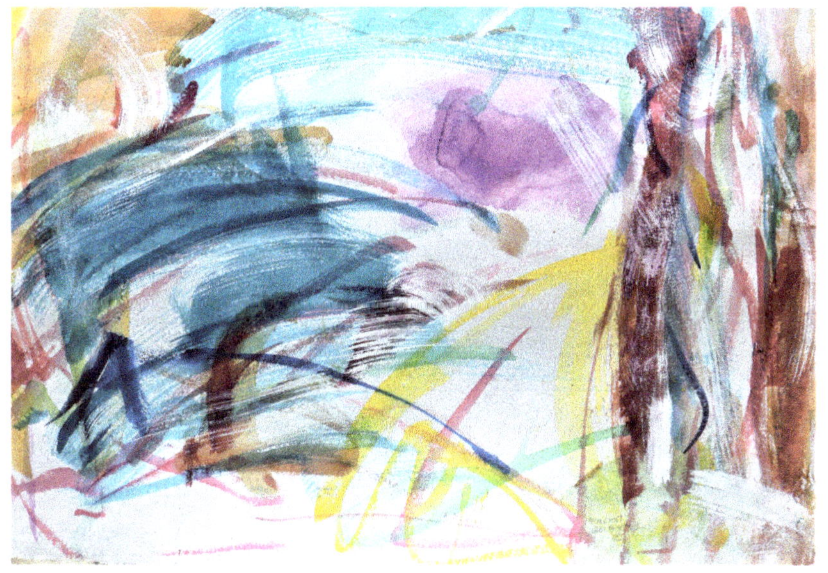

Boltzmann's Arrow

The arrow flies a simple course;
Unable to reverse its flight,
Or turn away from where it's aimed
Through gleaming day or hazy night.

It travels fast along our way
Exhorting us to hold the pace
Revealing what we need to do,
Imposing its unbending fate.

Can you hear it whistling by?
Graceful with its feathered shaft,
Seeking victims as it flies,
Towards a place of dying pasts.

Past decaying stumps and limbs,
Where victims crawl on bended knees
Toward the fringes of their lives,
Searching for safe symmetries.

To only sit is certain death;
But death is certain anyway.
Does it pay to race the wind
To some unknown infinity?

And yet the paradox, my friend,
Is life and death are mirrored selves
Of shadows which we cast away
On every journey to its end.

Take the one and find the other
Sitting down or lurking by—
A symbiosis, if you will,
Of nothingness and human cry.

Is it a game? I see no chance.
If no chance, why play at all?
Perhaps because we all are fools,
Perhaps to hear another call
Our hidden selves in ways of love,
So even as we meet our fate,
We should know that life was worth
The pain we had to tolerate.

When in the end the arrow falls
And time will lose its tyranny,
There's little more that we can choose
Except stay close to those we knew;
For what we did and how we loved
Will be reborn in memory.

The Start of a New Day

In the Kuzhmir Cemetery

Behind a wall of lives
Engraved in stones,
Searching for the homes
They left behind,
The Jews of Kuzhmir find
Instead the fissure in my heart.

Listen to their song!
Spun from breathless wind,
Weaving through the trees
In waltz time and sunshine.
It climbs the scales to heaven,
Rising in crescendo to a small
Still point where all is silent-
A rest note held forever.

Birch and pine bough,
Rustling "Amen"
To a Kaddish never said.
A song without words,
A nigun without Jews,
Except those whose souls
Are in the trees.

A song unfinished for the dead.

Rising to the Sky

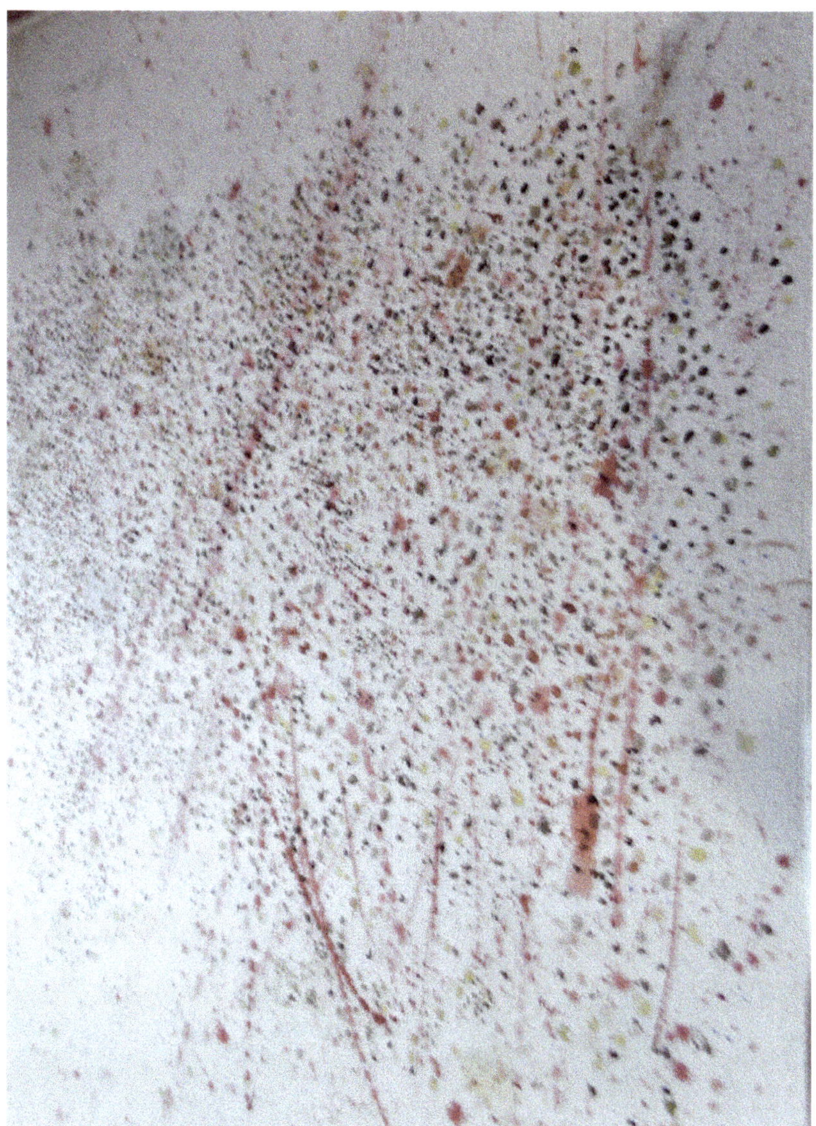

For Batya

Like water you are.
Cool and refreshing,
Hard to hold
Between my fingers,
Slipping through my grasp
To distant lands
Where you might mold
Yourself in forms
Both new and old.

Always moving,
Always flowing,
Toward an unknown plane
Where waits a
Small still pond
Refracting crystal light
From Heaven's sun
To hues the color
Of the rainbow.

And there beyond
The reach of gravity,
The headlong rush transforms
To eddies busy with
The gentle swirls of life,
At peace at last,
Content to know
The flow of love.

Falling Leaves

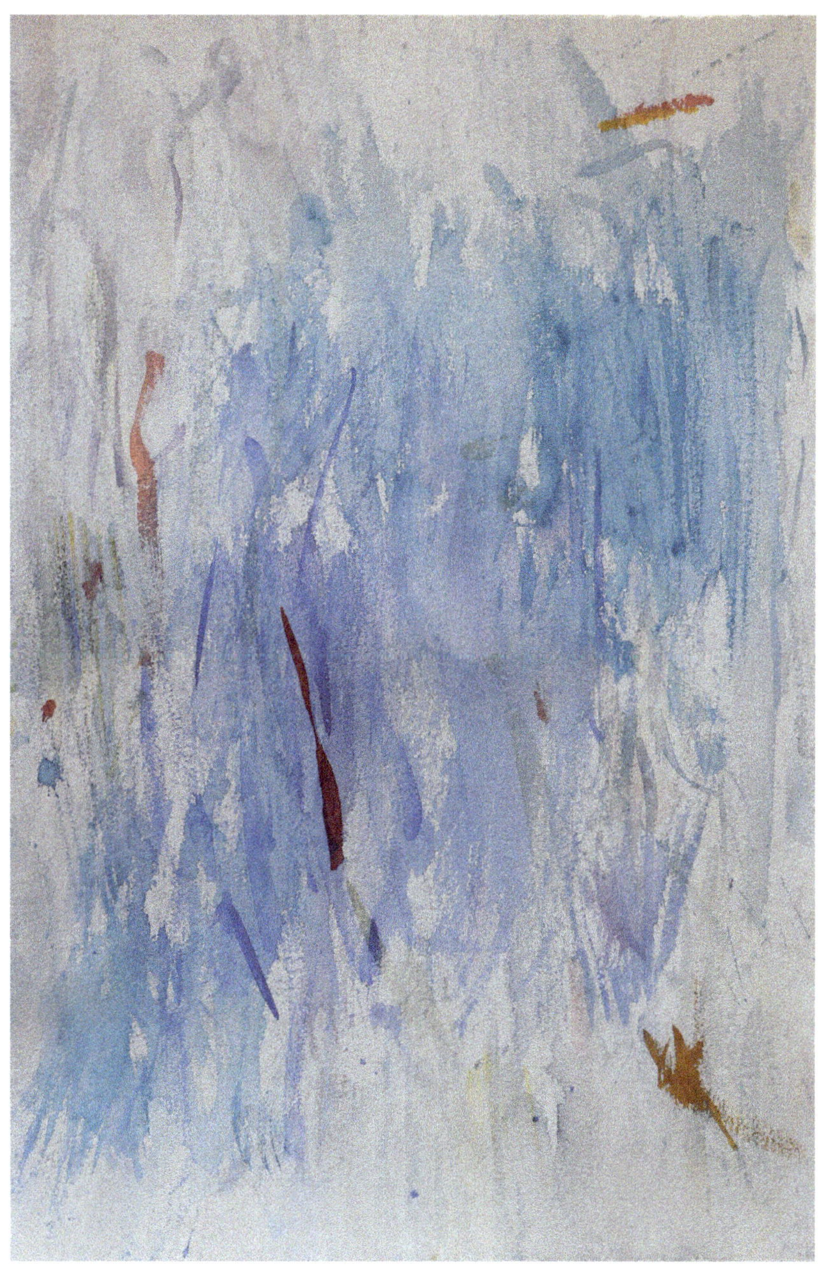

Eulogy for Maxi Blum

Though Maxi spoke in quiet tones
With gestures made of measured size,
The world would not contain his light,
Which blazed much wider than the flight
A comet makes on moonless nights.

Before he died he gave his heart ,
Heavy as the throbbing sea,
And in return received a gift,
As weightless as the summer breeze.

Across the vastness of the night
Conjured up by memory
He rides on top that gentle wind
Stretching out across the sky,
Reaching back to find alive
Those of us he left behind.

The gift he keeps and yet we have.
What was once will always be.
What is lost is somehow saved.
For love is stronger than the grave.

Contemplation (Brown)

Commencing Prayer on Sabbath Morning

Between the edge of Earth and Sky
The men assembled by and by
To wrap themselves in fringed Talit.

Folding high the wings of wool
Around their heads, each hides his face
And mutters blessings in cacophony.
Then mounting high their Pegasus of faith,
They ride and guide the aires of ancient prayers,
Through varied paths, their ways to Heaven's gate

Morning Prayer

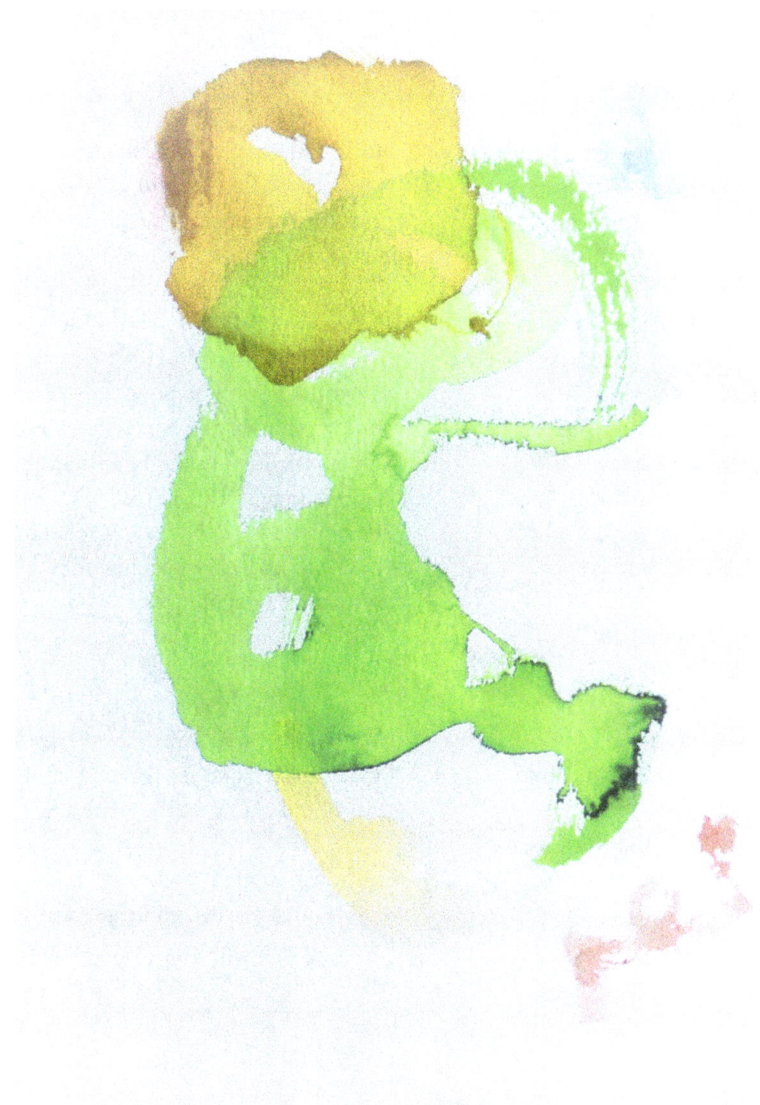

A Hike

Morning began as oft it will
With shimmering dew upon the grass
The smell was sweet with no decay-
A wonderful way to start a day.

Without another thought in mind
I planned to take a joy filled hike
Along the ridge and up the hill
Until I reached its topmost height
Where I could see what lay below
And revel in a broadened view
That might reveal the way I walked
And all the places I could go.

But halfway up I saw a path
Meandering to a lovely glen,
Hedged by flowers all around,
A quiet pond upon its end.
Lilies bloomed there pink and gold,
And woven in its grassy plot,
Like children playing hide and seek,
Were pretty blue forget-me-nots .

I took that path and settled down
Inside a spot that I found.
And from my pocket I grabbed a pen
With paper scraps I carried then
Of a half-done poem that would not yield
The sense of passions I could feel.

As word by word my poem took shape,
Through minute gaps, the hours flowed.
Though incomplete, as it grew late,
I stopped my work and rose to go.
But since the light had now grown dim,
There was no use in pushing on;
Afraid that I might lose my way,
I walked to where I had begun.

I never reached that summer peak
Nor saw the earth from eagles' eyes;
I made that trade with no complaints,
And would gladly do the same again.

But now that night is closing in,
And winds from distant heights still blow,
I wonder what there might have been
On all those paths I did not go.

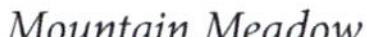

Mountain Meadow

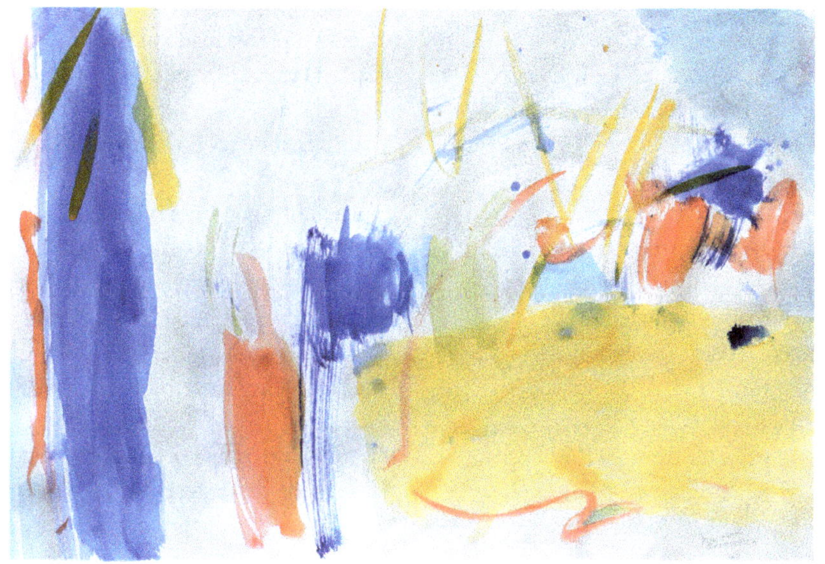

Metalurgy

Material Science

With sufficient time and heat
A flame can soften steel enough
To flow in rivers red as blood.
And adding just a touch of earth and sea,
Can make it stronger than a lover's
Sweet caress perceived in memory.
But if the heat is spent too fast,
The cold clear air will quench
The surface of the alloyed ore
And make it brittle to the touch
Until the tiny flaws, first formed
By furnace and by flame,
Break and shatter through the core,
Like love imposed upon a human heart.

Welding

Take two pieces made of steel.
Place them side by side like lovers in the night.
Grind their edges down until the ins and outs
Of each fit tight; then fuse them where they kiss
With spark and flame, until their essence
Has been mixed. A bond thus formed
Is stronger than the parent strain.
And there they stay, conjoined for all eternity,
Or until corrosion born of stress and time
Has changed the steel to rust
And broken through the trust
That bound the two as one,
Dissolving without pity
The union they had made.

Masque

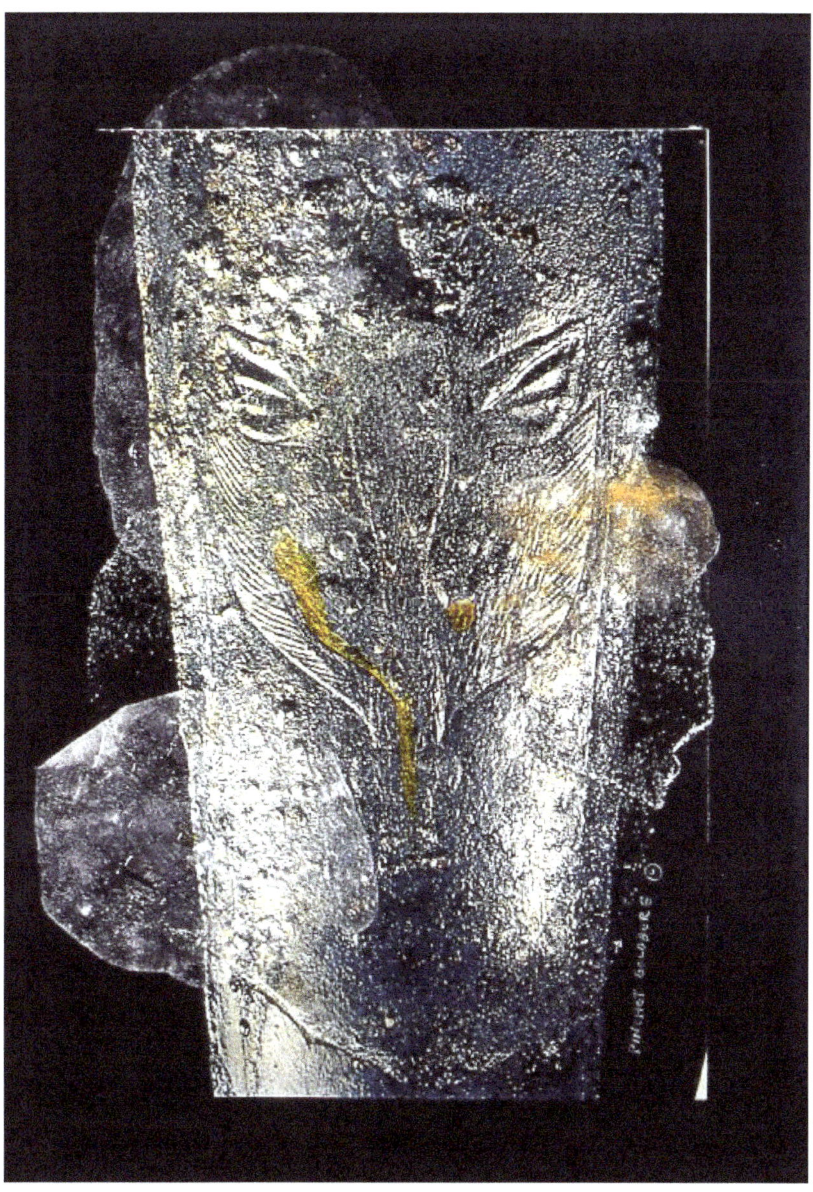

The Neighbor

My neighbor died the other day
Of causes which I cannot say I knew.
For forty years we lived across the street
And shared a view of falling leaves
In autumn's time, as well as budding trees
When spring would come around
With all those sounds of souciant birds
That sing unloved in peaceful towns.

And if by chance we got to meet
Amid the dance of daily chores,
We never knew quite what to say
Beyond a friendly loose limbed wave,
Or quickly said, "How goes the day?"

In time we saw each other age;
Our hair grew grey and health declined,
But still we never spoke the thoughts
That truly weighed upon our minds.

And yet I think that I will miss
Her presence in my clouded sight,
Her wraith like form across our street,
That shuffled through abrasive nights.

Surfing past the darkened seas,
She's cast upon some sifting shore,
Scrubbed translucent by the sand,
To disappear and be no more.

The Neighbor

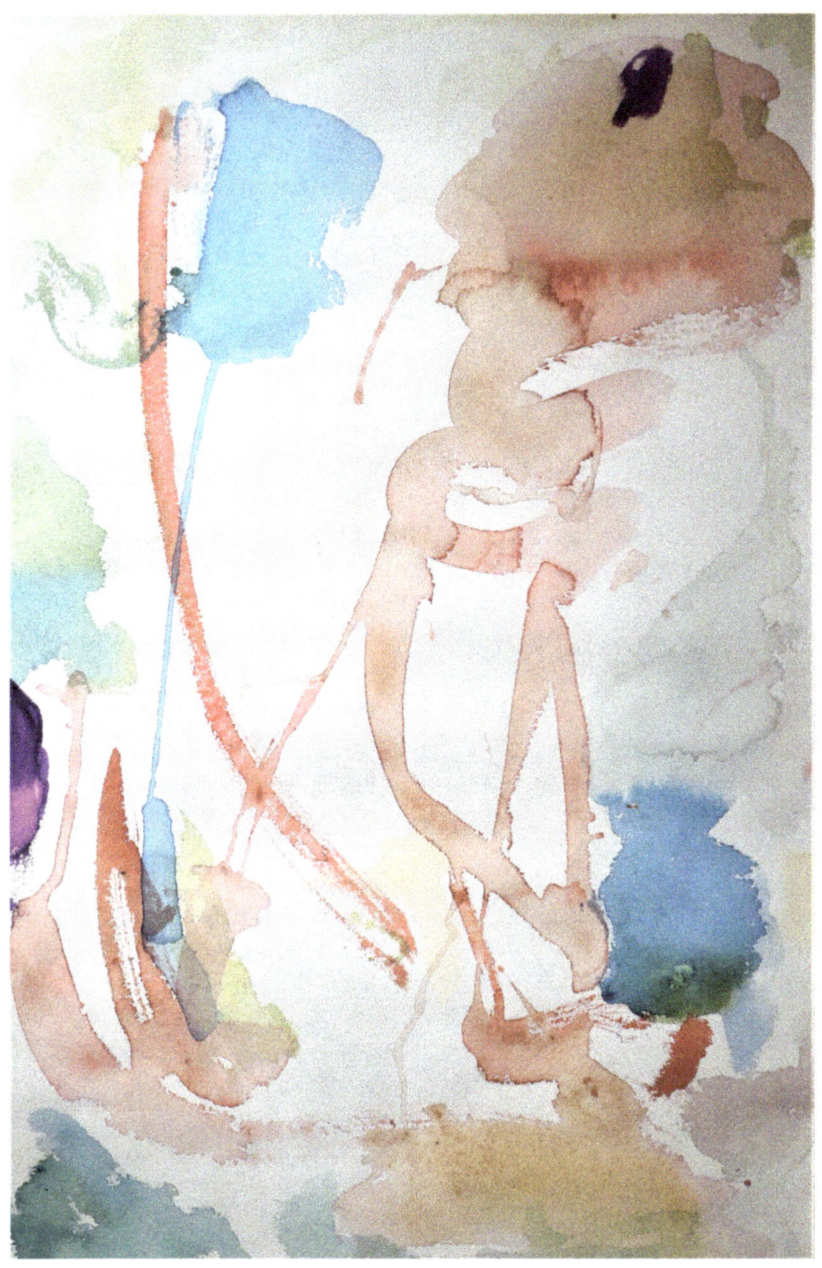

Korach's Lament

Weep for me departed friends,
Cry for me my love,
I shall never see again
The heavens bright above.

On solid ground I took my stand
To challenge earth and sky,
To let us live as we might choose
Without these laws and lies.

Why obey a prophecy that
Has us wander aimlessly,
Amid the sand and baking sun,
Until the day we die?

Was I wrong in what I said?
No longer slaves, but free,
I hoped with you at my command,
With Moses' power in our hands,
That we could leap our destiny
And shake death's dark decree.

A crevice formed beneath my feet,
As fear within me swelled,
I felt my body start to sway,
Into the hole I fell.

When Earth began to cease its yawn,
I found myself entombed,
Within this darkened sepulcher
That has become my home.

All around me blackness reigns.
My eyes no longer see
The colors and the shapes of life
That once delighted me.

But in their place another light
Has helped me to perceive
Grey shadows of a different world
Amid G-d's mysteries.

My hubris was a grievous sin.
I did not understand
That there are things
That cannot change,
No matter what we say.

Even though you wish to rage,
Remember this, my friends,
When after all our debts are paid,
That G-d still owns the day.

Weep for me departed friends,
Cry for me my love,
I shall never see again
The heavens bright above.

Weeping at Hormah

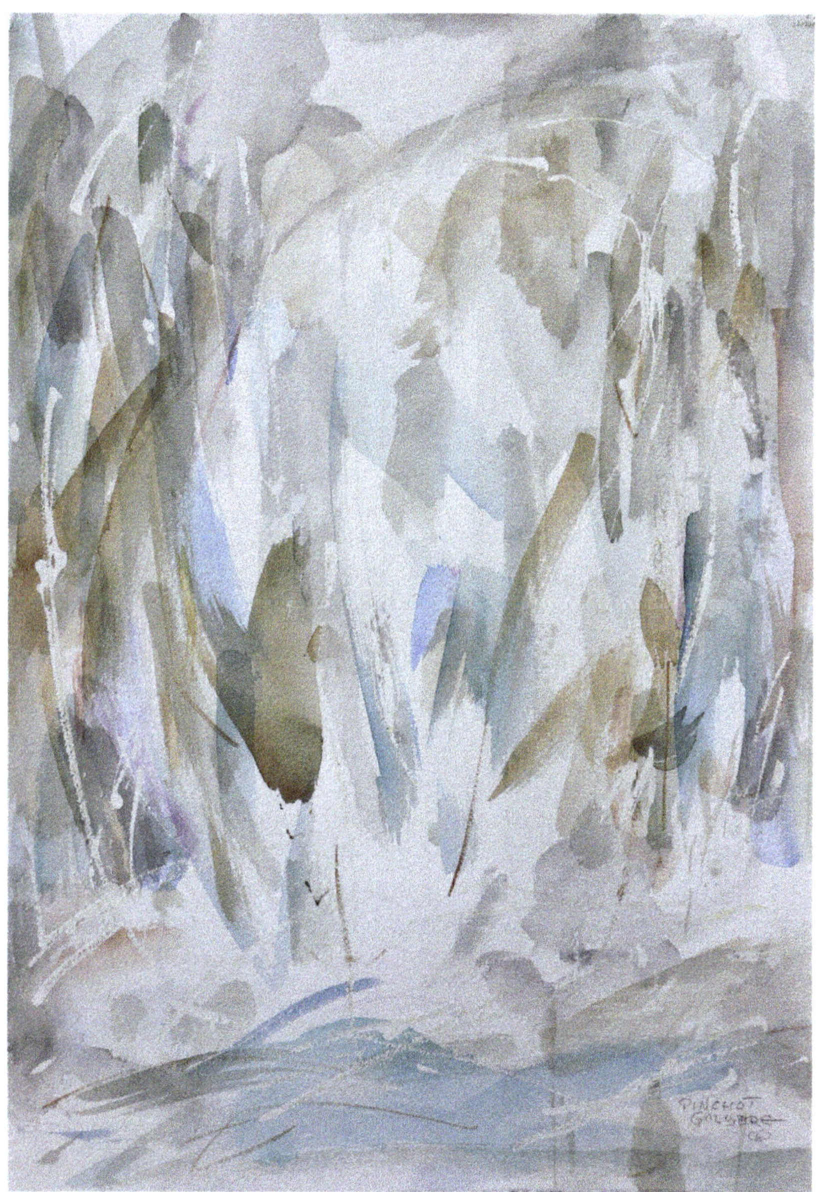

Memorial Day

The weather was warm for a late May day,
The sky was grey and threatened rain;
Normally I would have stayed at home,
But guilt encouraged me on my way
To visit graves of those I'd known.

So I drove in silence to where they lay
In a cemetery outside of town,
A pleasant place, if not for death,
Where one might picture children's play.

But the dead were there, and all around,
Their memories upon me pressed,
As frail as wisp around my head,
Like stone they lay upon my chest.

I moved among the many plots
Where neat brass markers broke the grass
To reveal the spot where someone lay,
Inside some dark and loamy space.

Father, mother, brothers two,
An uncle, niece, assorted friends
Were sown beneath that rolling ground,
Their bones in place and souls unbound.

I wished to know where they had gone
And of their thoughts of who I'd been,
And ask forgiveness for the wrongs
I'd done by small and major sins.

Despite the fights which sometimes raged,
I wished to feel their love again
To know the comfort of their kiss,
The sweet embrace they held me in.

I wanted us together then,
Vital as when all alive,
To inhale the smells of fertile dirt,
And feel the warmth of golden skies.

But silence reigned that cloudy day.
Their answers, muffled by their bones,
Would have to wait that other day
When I come back once more to stay.

So sensing that our time was up
With nothing more that might be known,
I took my leave of those I loved,
And journeyed back to town.

Memory of Light

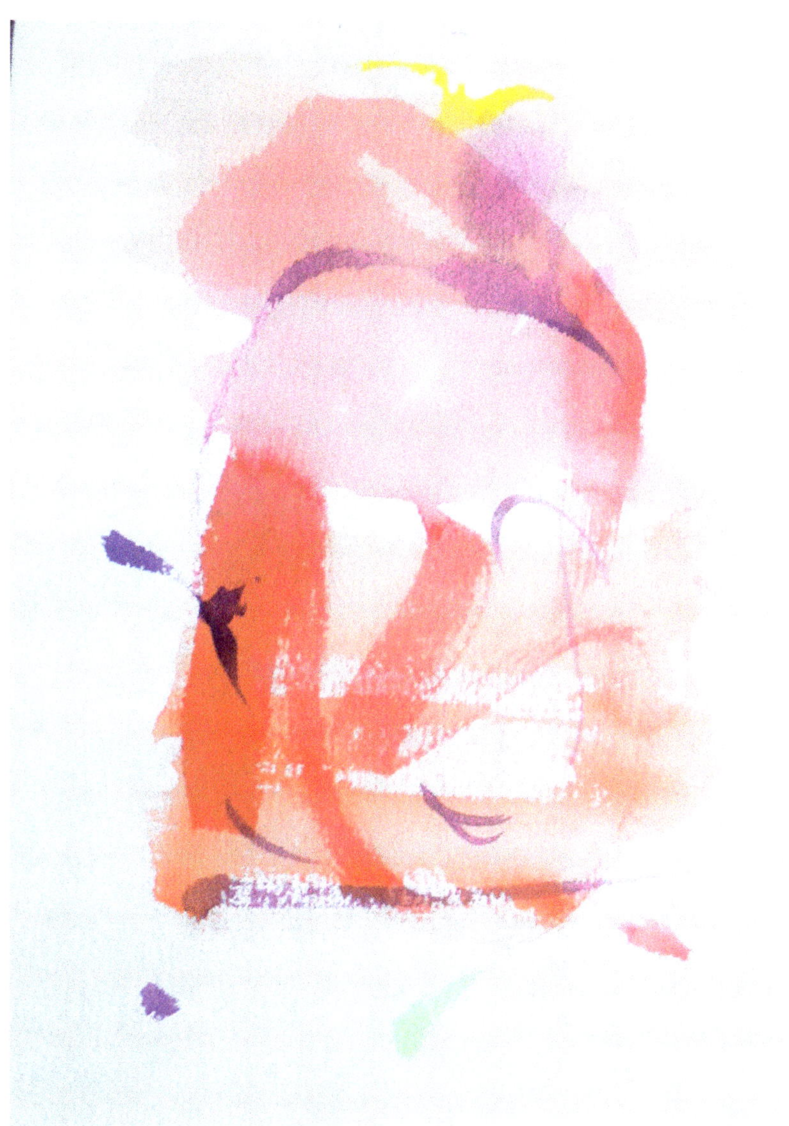

Puzzle

The world is made of little blocks
Of slate and marble, rock and stone,
Puzzled pieces interlocked
Of what is hidden, what is shown.
Place the like ones both together,
His to hers will make a whole;
If we have to question whether,
He and she must go alone.
Light reflected blue and green,
Below the surface less to see;
We cannot love what can't be found,
Or even know what it might mean.

The shape of voids are always changing,
Add a part, but lose the hole,
Find the answer to the puzzle,
Behold, another puzzle grows.
When the outside is completed,
Central parts will shape the key;
Test the many sided fragments.
Which is you, and where is me?

Always changing, never done;
Always many, always one.
The puzzle is but ours on lease,
Quickly find another piece!

Searching

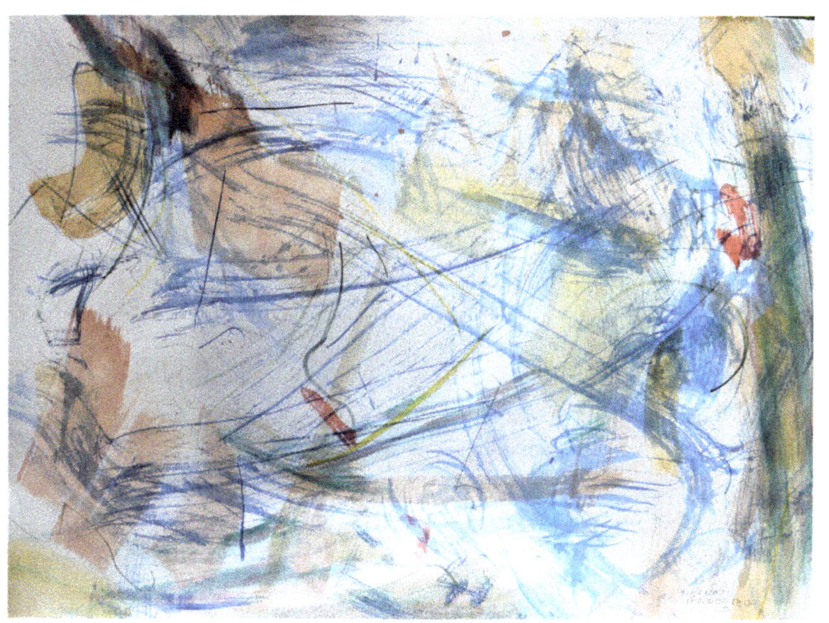

The Wind and the Slaves

When Death became the wind at night
Below a moon of early spring,
It slithered through the masters' homes
To find and kill their first offspring.

But for the slaves the wind bequeathed
A freedom they could not conceive;
A life that's free from lash and pain,
Was all they wanted to receive.

Now with seven days gone by,
The waves had stopped their journey short,
Confused, they faltered near the shore
Unsure of what the day might bring.
But through the whirling dust they saw
Egyptians formed in quick pursuit
To seize the men who had escaped
And make them grovel once again.

Their faith, so small and grimly gained,
Was lost amid the noise and fears.
Their questioning gave voice to dread,
"Perhaps a sin it was to dream,
Or perhaps much worse", or so it seemed,
"To cling to hope and still believe."

As they lingered on the shore,
Frozen in their clinging doubt,
The strong East wind at morning's light,
Cold and cruel as Pharaoh's Heart,
Peering deep in memory,
Remembered why it had to be—
And waiting but a moment more,
Rose in rage and cleaved the sea.

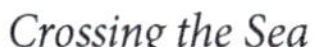

Crossing the Sea

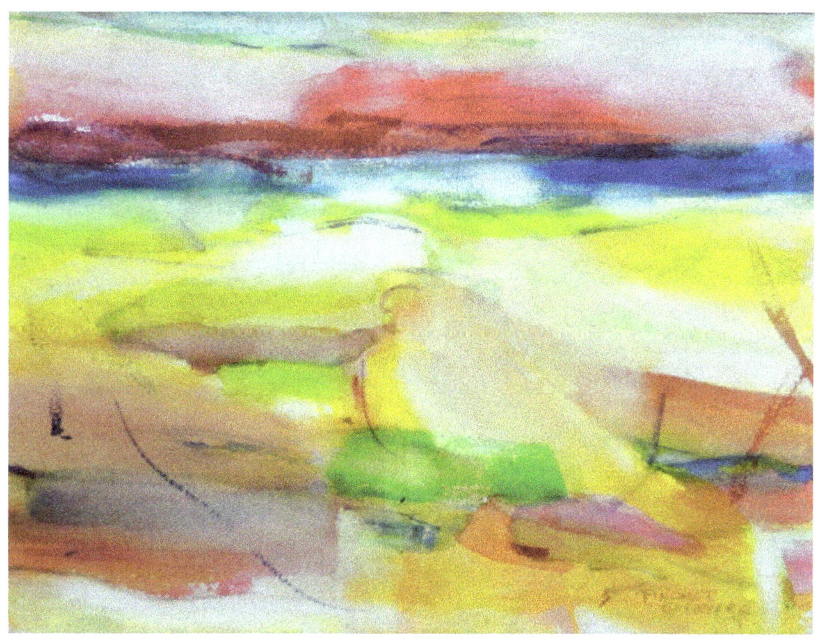

Eldad and Medad

Elders to what had been slaves,
Amid the early morning damp
We sat and listened to complaints,
Of what they wanted, what we lacked.
The food was sparse, they wanted more.
The manna was too bland to bear.
They hungered for a little meat,
And feared the life that they would share.

With bodies free, but souls enchained
The wretched men could not conceive,
The joy and pride to be one's own,
The hope that comes from being free.

They wanted still the life they'd known
Without the need of pride or shame,
The patterns of a well worn day,
Where past and future were the same.
A simple place, with choices few,
Though driven by a whipping hand,
Where each man knew what he must do,
A life that all could understand.

"Why believe?" The rebels sneered,
"We cannot see this G-d of ours,
Nor ever hear what He has said,
Or even know if He is here.
Is He foe or is He friend? Perhaps
He'll make us slaves again."

What of this man who leads us now,
Who claims the voice of prophecy?
"It is our G-d", the man has said,
"Who brought us up from slavery,
Who fought our battle at the sea,
Who guarantees to keep us fed."

But now he seeks a distant place;
He says, "It is the promised land."
But no one knows what we might find,
Whether paradise or graves of sand.

To gain the elders' sympathy
He summoned us to share his sight,
But scared of what we thought might be,
And lacking reasons to agree,
We choose to hide inside the camp,
Wrapped safely in obscurity.

But plans like men oft go astray,
And what we wish might never be.
So words unbid, against our wills,
Began to swirl inside our heads
With visions of a vast abyss
Beyond the living and the dead.

They showed us much of what might be—
Of hope amid our loss and ruin,
But terror too engulfed our hearts
As we perceived Infinity.

Too much we saw and understood,
Deceived no more by petty lies,
Eternity before us lay,
As we began to prophesy.

That is all and nothing more.
We finally saw what he could see
And understood what he must bear,
This burden brought of prophecy.
The words and visions came and went
And we appear much as before
Except the memory of that time
Has changed our souls forevermore.

No more we wonder what to do,
Of what is wrong and what is right.
We understand that all is G-d,
Be it darkness, be it light.
The Truth is not a simple thing;
It makes us slaves; it makes us free.
A curse to know what need occur,
This blessed gift of clarity.

Pavilion Screen

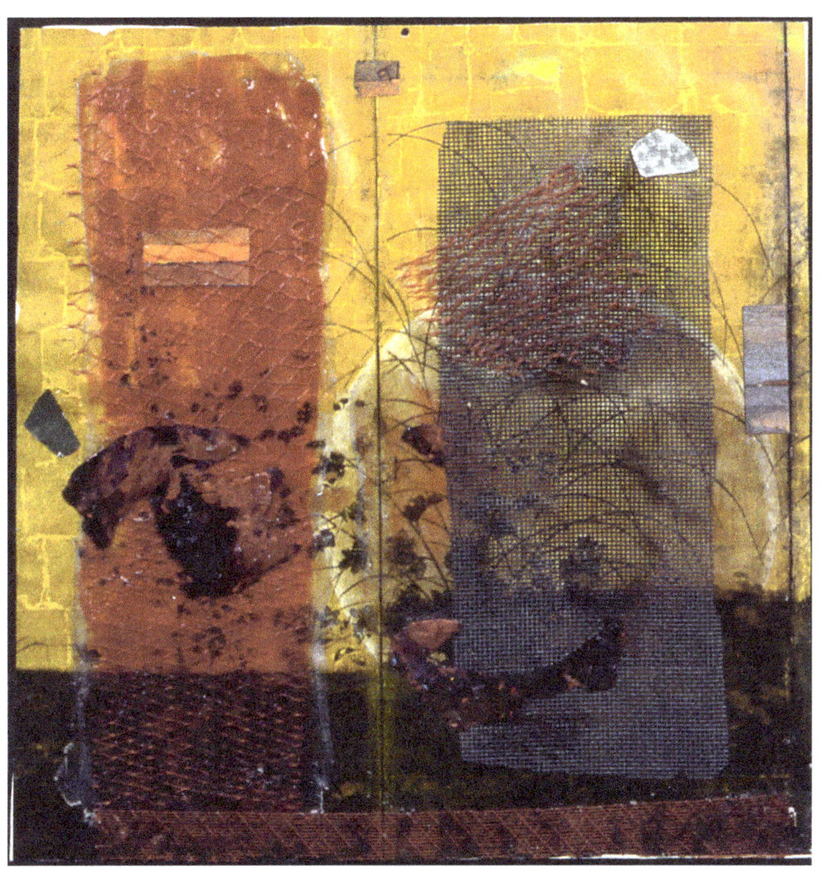

Young Love

When I was young and I could hate
My loving took a fearsome shape.
For when my love would go unheard
I raged at fate and cursed that world
Which would not listen to my words.

Love unheard was love denied
And it could shape a hate inside
To poison both a soul and mind
Until all love might dissipate,
Transfigured into fearsome hate.

To live with love was to love a lie
As normal hearts cannot survive
Too many cuts by sharpened tongues,
Or loss of blood when love had fled
To other loves in other beds.

I learned to shrink this awful love,
To ease that site of greatest pain,
While hate, withdrew in sympathy,
And lost its great control of me.

And I am better for that change.

Upon my heart a scar has formed
Above the wounds of love and hate,
Yet still I see on frigid nights
The small faint sight of distant lights
Formed from bright and blazing fires
And feel the embers of desire.

Young Love

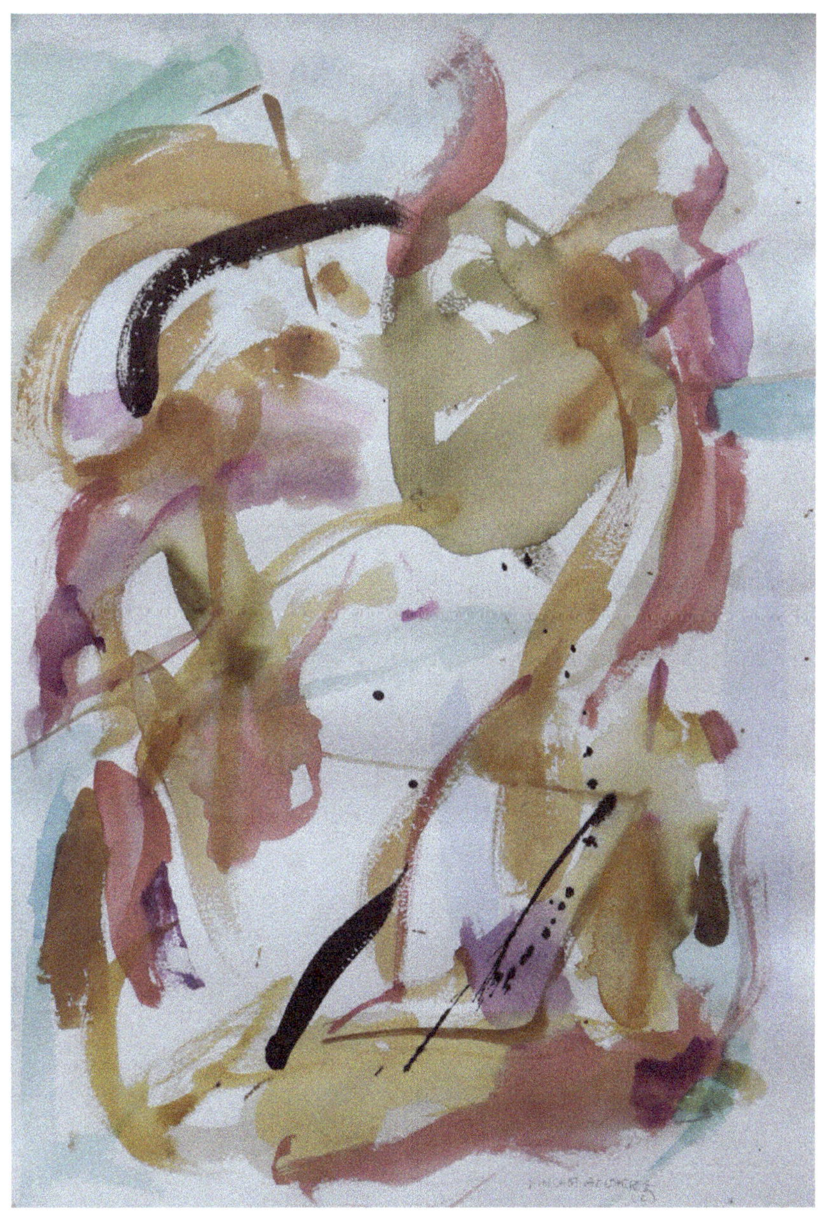

Questions

I wish to know what is in store
For me when I'm no longer here;
Beyond the life of flesh and bone,
Beyond the life I've always known.

What awaits behind that veil?
Is it Heaven? Is it Hell?
Perhaps a dark and lonely space
From which I cannot find escape.

Will I remember who I've been?
Did my life mean anything,
Or was it just a vacant dream,
A shadow passing from the scene?

And if by chance my soul survives
What does it mean that it's alive?
Will I see all those I'd loved?
And know their futures from above?

Will Earthly voices trouble me?
Will I hear their anguished cries
Or sounds of joy from happy times
By those my death has left behind?

Will I find myself with G-d?
Will I know that all is right?
Perhaps I'll find a peaceful sleep
Knowing that my life's complete.

Beyond the Veil

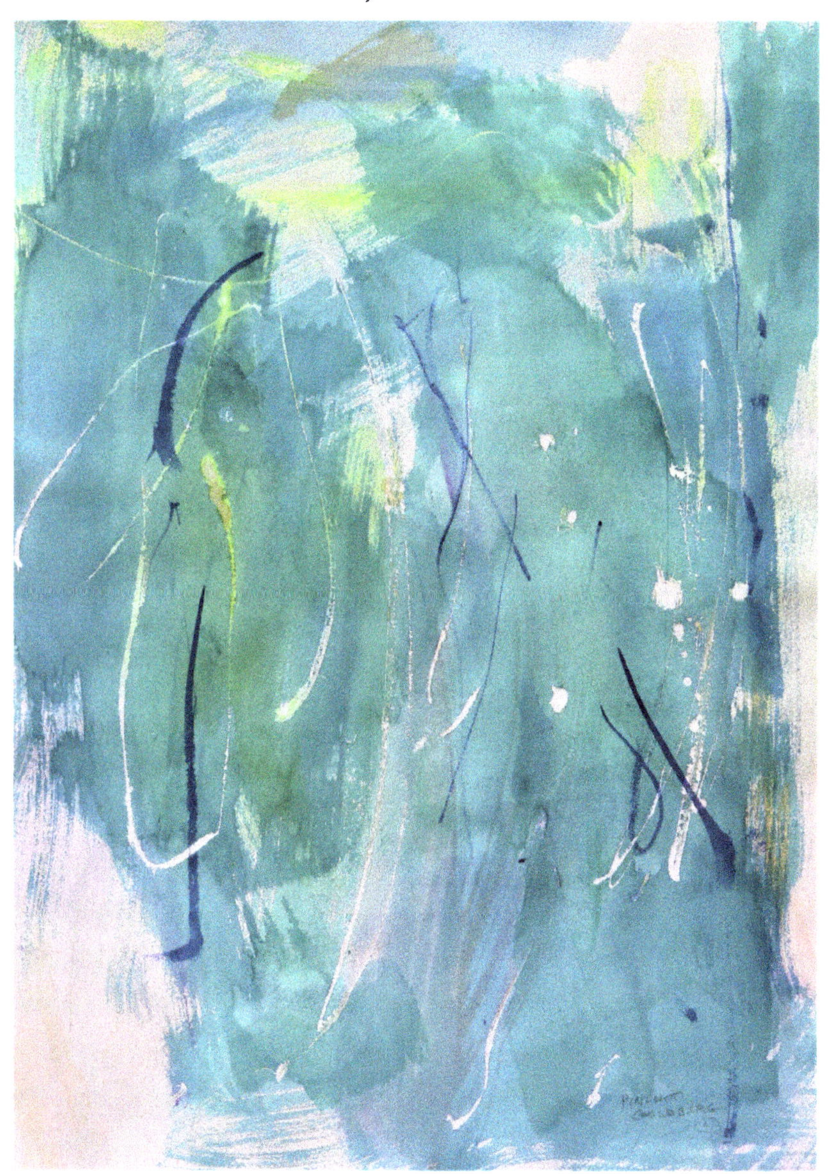

A Young Man's Lament

Tomorrow I will thank you for your self-control,
To stop the passion far before the sin.
But not today. Because today I want
To hear your gentle voice which
Echoes through the trees,
Scented with the perfumed air
Of lilacs in the spring.

And tomorrow I will see my error clear,
Of how I could have ruined my life
And lost my soul. But not today.
Because today I want to feel the aura
Of your smile which warms my heart
As I begin my day.

And tomorrow I will know that I was wrong to ask
What should not be. But not today.
Because today I want to see you
Standing here before me, graceful
As a faun with wonder in your eyes.

And tomorrow I may think you never were-
A phantom of my mind which I had conjured up
From books and dreams. But not today.
Because today I can no longer dream
The dreams of what might be.
And in my heart I feel an emptiness.

Confusion in Love

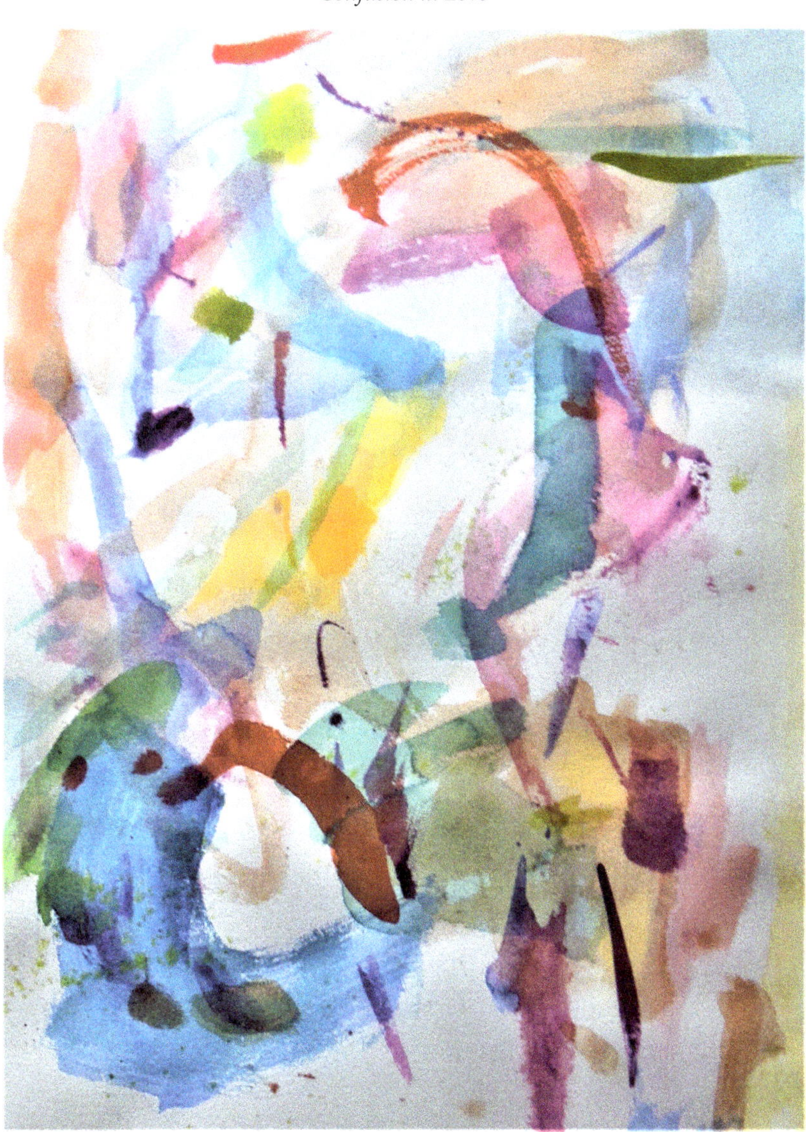

www.ingramcontent.com/pod-product-compliance
Lightning Source LLC
LaVergne TN
LVHW050540100826
845148LV00002B/632

* 9 7 8 1 7 2 5 2 6 8 5 1 7 *